DAV
MENTOR

DAWOOD'S MENTOR

THE MAN WHO MADE INDIA'S BIGGEST DON

S. HUSSAIN ZAIDI

An imprint of Penguin Random House

EBURY PRESS

USA | Canada | UK | Ireland | Australia
New Zealand | India | South Africa | China

Ebury Press is part of the Penguin Random House group of companies
whose addresses can be found at global.penguinrandomhouse.com

Published by Penguin Random House India Pvt. Ltd
7th Floor, Infinity Tower C, DLF Cyber City,
Gurgaon 122 002, Haryana, India

First published in Ebury Press by Penguin Random House India 2019

10 9 8 7 6 5 4 3 2 1

This book is a work of non-fiction and is based on the evidence collected from a variety of sources, interviews conducted and personal interactions of the author with the various persons mentioned in the book. The views and opinions expressed in the chapters of this book are those of the author only and do not reflect or represent the views and opinions held by any other person.

This book is based on actual events and is based on evidence collected by the author with respect to the events enumerated. It reflects the author's representation of the events enumerated as truthfully as possible on the basis of the interviews conducted with various individuals and/or on the basis of materials that can be verified by research. All persons within the book are actual individuals.

The objective of this book is not to hurt any sentiments or be biased in favour of or against any particular person, society, gender, creed, nation or religion.

ISBN 9780143425977

Typeset in Adobe Jenson Pro by Manipal Digital Systems, Manipal
Printed at Thomson Press India Ltd, New Delhi

www.penguin.co.in

With love,
For Rayyan Shabeeb Rizvi

Contents

Acknowledgements

Everyone is my teacher
Some I seek
Some I subconsciously attract
Often, I learn simply
By observing others
Some may be completely unaware that
I am learning from them
Yet, I bow deeply in gratitude.

—Anonymous

A man's mettle, his character and the choices he makes in life all boil down to having a great mentor. The ones who make their mark in life always talk about the people who shaped their minds, forged their thoughts and perspectives and carved their personality; they talk of the people and books that left an indelible impression on their minds. A mentor is the architect of a man's character and the sculptor of his personality. A mentor could be your parent, spouse, sibling, teacher, friend or even a colleague at work. The only prerequisites for the pupil is that s/he needs to have cognizance of the mentor's presence in his or her life and that s/he needs to deeply respect the mentor and possess a deep hunger to follow and emulate the mentor.

In the Mahabharata, Eklavya was denied tutelage by Dronacharya, but his burning desire to excel and follow the teacher made him a better archer than Arjun. The warrior in Arjun attained his peak of perfection only when his friend—who was also his charioteer—Krishna decided to mentor him in Kurukshetra.

Before Moses embarked on his mission to take on the might of the Pharaoh, it was Jethro who coached and trained him. Moses ended up marrying Jethro's daughter after serving him for years.

Both Christianity and Islam emphasize on servitude and humility to the mentor. Jesus showed the way through humility and often led by example. Prophet Muhammad's most devout disciple was his cousin Ali ibn Abi Talib, popularly known as Ali. The disciple was so humble before Muhammad that he would not even hesitate to cobble his master's shoes. Muhammad reciprocated with compassion and eventually had his daughter betrothed to Ali. The art of losing oneself while learning from the mentor makes one the best protégé. And the best protégé actually turns out to be the most effective mentor. Till date, Hazrat Ali's followers swear by his principles, integrity, valour, his exemplary character, his inner and outer strength and his loyalty to his mentor.

Dedicated learners and students pick up more wisdom from their mentors than from their own parents. Napoleon Hill met Andrew Carnegie a couple of times but was deeply influenced by him. Hill went on to write the bestselling book *Think and Grow Rich*, a bible for millions of entrepreneurs.

The book changed so many lives for the better—its happy beneficiaries swear by its pull and influence in their lives till today.

On the other hand, the mentor has so much tenacity and wisdom that he does not dwell on his protégé's turnabout. If Ernest Hemingway was mentored by Sherwood Anderson, Hemingway did not reciprocate. Flush with arrogance, Hemingway ridiculed Anderson in a satire after achieving fame. But Sherwood Anderson was unfazed and continued grooming talents. American writers like William Faulkner and F. Scott Fitzgerald emerged from the Anderson stable.

Speaking of mentors, I would like to share my own personal story as an example for all my students. At seventeen, I was gauche and lacked in confidence. I was trying to complete my education even as I was trying to support my parents by working part-time. As my written and spoken English left a lot to be desired, I was very embarrassed. One day I was sitting, forlorn, in a library in suburban Mumbai, wondering how I could improve my writing skills. Suddenly, a youth, probably the same age as me, who was aware of my problems, walked up to me and, after a brief dialogue, offered me a book—*Not a Penny More, Not a Penny Less* by Jeffrey Archer.

I first met Shabeeb Rizvi several years ago during lunch at a common friend's place and had not taken much of a liking to him. He was talking about various books and his command over English was superb. I misinterpreted his knowledge and his suaveness. I thought that because he was the scion of a prominent family in Bandra, he was flaunting his social status. Actually, I carried this resentment against him for quite some time. But that day in the library, we forged a bond that remains strong till date.

I remember his first piece of advice: 'The best way to master a language is to read the masters of that language excessively.' That was the beginning. I voraciously devoured thrillers and other assorted pulp fiction, essentially whatever I could lay my hands on—Frederick Forsyth, Ian Fleming, Robert Ludlum, Ken Follett, David Baldacci, David Morrell, John Grisham, Scott Turow, Steve Martini, Sidney Sheldon, Irwin Wallace and their contemporary thriller writers. At one point of time, the bookstall owners at Fort and Kala Ghoda started recognizing me and sweetly keeping copies of various books for me. Needless to say, I began to absorb from these master storytellers. I ended up reading hundreds of books and I would like to say that those books did for me what no creative-writing classes could do for an eager student.

When I became closer to Shabeeb Sir, I discovered so many facets to him that I realized that my initial assessment of him stemmed from an inferiority complex—he was everything that I was not. The man was a polyglot and could speak over half a dozen languages with equal ease and felicity. He devoured books on various subjects like a carnivore pouncing on its prey. He read everything that he could lay his hands on. He had an insatiable appetite for books. He read history, philosophy and logic, grammar, dictionaries and lexicons—anything that fancied him. Shabeeb Sir is a man of many parts, a speaker, researcher, writer, translator, analyst and the author of over 200 treatises, dissertations and research topics, not to mention that he is responsible for the translation of several iconic Arabic books into English. I was also intrigued by his way of living, which was spartan, to say the least. There was nothing ostentatious about him or his lifestyle despite his family's wealth. I was also charmed by his magnanimity. I learnt valour, integrity, humility, fearlessness and selflessness from him.

I began to look up to him as my first mentor. He taught me to make a lot of money and spend it generously on family and friends and, after them, on have-nots like widows, orphans and the poor. He believed there was no point in hoarding money like misers do, because one won't be able to take it to the grave.

Shabeeb Sir and I grew up together; his keen interest in academics led him to pursue a doctorate in a business subject. As for me, I veered off into the export–import business before finding my feet in journalism. But I did not lose touch with Shabeeb Sir. I was picking up a lot of things from him, even things he never taught me. I met him regularly, at least once every week, and imbibed some of those monklike characteristics that keeps one solid from the inside.

In my job as a crime reporter, I dealt with criminals and blood and murder. To see all that and still remain unaffected takes a lot of effort. I learnt not to be afraid of the mafia or their diktats, not to get intimidated either by power, the government or reckless police officers. It was my years of association with Dr Shabeeb Rizvi that made me the man I eventually became—both in my mind and spirit. If God had not sent a Shabeeb Rizvi into my life, I would have been just another young man spending decades in the pursuit of elusive success.

Ten years after meeting Dr Shabeeb 'The Superb' Rizvi, I met my second mentor in life, Vikram 'The Great' Chandra. Vikram was already a globally acclaimed author of several bestselling books but it was his extreme humility that touched a chord with me. Vikram had met dozens of journalists but he decided to befriend me. We had met when he was researching his acclaimed book *Sacred Games*, now a popular series on Netflix. We both went to various shady places and survived so many risky adventures. Vikram was good at decrypting men of all hues. He took very scant notes but clicked pictures of the surroundings with his mental camera. Often his face was ashen due to his intense effort at absorbing the minutest of details, for instance, at the den of Karim Lala or at Dagdi Chawl or outside Pakmodia Street, which was the hub of Dawood Ibrahim's gang. I devoted a lot of my reporting time to him as I was learning again with him. Vikram insisted on compensating me handsomely for my time and effort, but I refused point-blank.

It was Vikram who introduced me to Penguin Books and exhorted me to write. My debut book, *Black Friday*, is the result of Vikram's lessons to me about storytelling and crafting an interesting narrative. To date, this is my favourite book.

A person is the sum total of lessons s/he has acquired from several teachers and mentors, but only a few remain special and memorable to him. For me, Shabeeb Sir and Vikram Chandra were life-changing universities that gave me the best education.

To give back what one has acquired is a prerequisite of gratitude. My first-ever protégé was Rayyan Rizvi, Shabeeb Sir's eldest son. I have known Rayyan since his birth and I instantly fell in love with him the moment I saw him.

Soon after completing his college education Rayyan joined the *Asian Age* as an intern, when I was the resident editor of the Mumbai edition. He was keen on pursuing a career in journalism but the compulsions of family businesses took him away from his aspirations and he ended up handling the Dubai branch of his flourishing business. Rayyan relocated to Dubai soon after and we lost touch.

When I needed Rayyan's help in Dubai, I knocked on his door and he was very generous with his time and money. This book would not have been possible without Rayyan's contribution. His devotion, dogged perseverance and immense research skills helped me in culling out the authentic details of Dubai as a city. Rayyan was also present with me during Khalid's extensive interviews and meticulously took notes, often rushing to the spot at short notice without even having breakfast.

Apart from Rayyan, I came across two other men whose devotion, affection and hunger to learn was immensely inspiring. Gautam Mengle, a nervous, diffident young man who met me at the *Asian Age* and made his debut as a crime reporter in 2008. I decided to try him out first and asked him to work without a salary for the first ten days. The man really worked hard and earned his stripes. On 1 September 2008, he was hired as trainee reporter, and then 26/11 happened. It was too soon for a reporter who was still wet behind the ears, but he really rose to the challenge and, like a solid crime journo, did a wonderful job of reporting on the biggest terrorist attack in Mumbai. Today, after ten years, Gautam can be easily listed among the top five crime reporters in the city.

Equally amazing is the rise of another pupil of mine. I met Bilal Siddiqi in 2013, when he was all of eighteen. I seriously did not want to take him under my wing. He was too tender and seemed vulnerable. I assigned him some near-impossible tasks which he somehow managed to finish with aplomb—and then asked for more! I was totally floored with that kind of attitude. In the last five years, Bilal has gone from strength to strength, authored three books and written a couple of scripts. Soon, Bilal's debut book with Penguin, *The Bard of Blood*, will be adapted into a web series on Netflix.

I am delighted to have these two men in my team who keep making me proud with their intelligent insights, their indefatigable diligence and their unswerving friendship to a man double their age. *Shukriya*, Gautam and Bilal.

Another protégé of mine who was of immense help with regard to this book was Iram Siddique. Iram is an intrepid reporter with the *Mumbai Mirror* and she often tried to strike a fine balance with her demanding daily reporting and my high expectations. She managed to achieve both. She was part of several interviews that I had with Sikandar Shah in coffee shops or at his house, and she accurately transcribed them all for me.

Yesha Kotak, a journo with *Hindustan Times,* was the first one to help me on this project when she started translating lot of documents from Hindi and English; she showed plenty of patience with me while fulfilling the tasks assigned to her. Yesha also helped me in taking notes and transcribing interviews as well.

Film-maker Sanjay Gupta is a superb storyteller. He can hold your attention for hours, and you will never get tired of listening to him with undiluted concentration. Sanjay was very forthcoming about his ordeal with regard to *Shootout at Wadala*. Thanks, Sanjay.

Among the police officers, Pradeep Sharma was of tremendous help. Sharma opened several closed and inaccessible doors that I faced during the research for the book. Thank you, Sharma Sahib.

Sachin Waze, a former police officer with the Mumbai crime branch, helped me in his own subtle and studious manner with plenty of documents and archives.

Zia Abbas Mirza provided his technical assistance and archived precious photographs. The man is superbly brilliant at his work and selfless in providing us sterling service in the wee hours of the morning, when it was needed most urgently.

A few members of the mafia were, as usual, very forthcoming, with a lot of valuable inputs but, of course, I cannot take names. They would not appreciate such a gesture.

Milee Ashwarya, my publisher at Penguin, is not just an editor or professional partner but also a close friend. She was a pillar of support during my time with the book. Thank you, Milee.

There are times when you have not someone in person but still that person feels so familiarly *apna* and close. I feel that with my editor, Rachita Raj. Rachita had earlier edited my book *Dangerous Minds* and ensured that it was so flawless that I began to entertain the thought that I was a good writer. Rachita is helpful, understanding, accommodating and a rare human being. Thanks, Rachita, I owe you big time.

Finally, I would like to convey my immeasurable gratitude to my wife and editor, Velly Thevar, who, surprisingly, was appreciative of the book. She fine-tuned the language glitches and made the narrative more muscular. Velly's reworking has enhanced the reading pleasure of the book. Often I slept peacefully because I knew that Velly was awake and working on improving the chapter. Thank you, Editor Sahiba.

List of Acronyms

ACP	Assistant commissioner of police
CID	Criminal Investigation Department
COFEPOSA	Conservation of Foreign Exchange and Prevention of Smuggling Activities Act
DCP	Deputy commissioner of police
DRI	Directorate of Revenue Intelligence
FIR	First Information Report
IPC	Indian Penal Code
IPS	Indian Police Service
MHADA	Maharashtra Housing and Area Development Authority
MISA	Maintenance of Internal Security Act
NSA	National Security Act
ROI	Return on Investment
RSP	Road Safety Patrol
SLR	Self-Loading Rifle
UAE	United Arab Emirates
USD	United States Dollar

1

The Pathan Threat

The barrel of the gun was pointed at Dawood Ibrahim's heart. The gunman had been training his focus for a long time. He was waiting for the right moment to pull the trigger. The gunman had only one chance. If the bullet missed the target, the man at the other end would certainly gift him a not-so-exquisite death.

The man pointing the muzzle at Dawood had been sent by his arch-rivals from the underworld. The gunman was accompanied by his cronies, who were huge, hefty men called the Pathans, with Peshawari and Afghan ancestry. Since the 1950s, the Pathans, known for their moneylending habits, had taken to crime. Cousins Amirzada and Alamzeb wanted Dawood dead. The man was a menace. An audacious chit of a boy, he challenged the Pathan hegemony, and since the time he had emerged in the area as a small-time criminal, was proving to be a headache for the Pathans.

In the 1970s, the turf war among the mob generally ended with some serious skirmishes. But the Pathans were so furious with the tenacious Dawood Ibrahim that they decided to investigate his sources of power. They found a nexus between local newspaper-owner and crime reporter Iqbal Natiq and Dawood. The two shared an amazing rapport, with Dawood invariably spending a couple of hours every day at Natiq's office in BIT Blocks in Dongri. And Natiq's newspaper—*Raazdaar* (The Confidante)—exposed the Pathans often, which brought the police to their doorstep.

As retribution, the Pathans killed Natiq brutally. Dawood and his brother Sabir Kaskar swore revenge. Their first target was Saeed Batla. They did not kill Batla, preferring, instead, to maim him and amputate his fingers, something unheard of in the Indian underworld in those times. Before they could proceed with such 'special treatment' for the other Pathans, the police picked them up. However, the Kaskar brothers managed to secure bail on attempt-to-murder charges.

Upon receiving bail, as is routine in any police prosecution case, Sabir and Dawood were supposed to intermittently present themselves at the Nagpada police station in central Bombay (now Mumbai). They had to assure the cops that they were not up to any mischief and that they were miles away from any criminal activities. The slang for these routine police-station visits is *haazari lagana* (marking one's attendance), where the accused meet the police inspector, answer a few questions and leave within a few minutes.

Dawood preferred the formality of the official haazari to the cold walls of the prison and, of course, it helped that these visits ensured that the police did not land up at their house and complain to their father, Ibrahim Kaskar, who was also a cop. Kaskar senior was an absolute disciplinarian who was known to reserve his leather-belt treatment for the unbridled Dawood, his third child.

On that cool afternoon in October 1980, a defenceless Dawood, along with Sabir, was the target. The Pathans—

Amirzada and Alamzeb—knew that Dawood would not be carrying any weapons to the police station. They decided to take advantage of this particular visit to finish off Dawood, because under no other circumstances would they find him unarmed.

But what they did not see coming was another Pathan, Khalid Khan, who shepherded Dawood to the police station that day. Built like a mountain, with a towering height of 6 feet 2 inches and a brawny physique, Khalid was very attached to the promising young Dawood.

Earlier, Khalid had cut his teeth in crime with another don, a local strongman by the name of Bashu Dada. But that was long before Dawood endeared himself to him. Khalid was very protective of Dawood, and that particular day his instincts told him that Dawood would be vulnerable and in a tight spot around the police station. He rationalized that since Nagpada was closer to Kamathipura and Tardeo, the stronghold of the Pathans, they might make a play for Dawood.

Khalid cancelled all his engagements scheduled for that day and decided to follow Dawood to the police station. He also decided to escort him back to his headquarters at Musafir Khana, safe and unharmed. Since Khalid's name was not in the First Information Report (FIR), he could safely accompany Dawood and also carry a weapon on the sly. The cops would not frisk him for weapons, he surmised.

After Dawood and Sabir signed their attendance and completed other formalities, they saluted the cops—there was a lot of respect for the uniform; it came from their father—and were on their way towards the exit.

They were oblivious to the face of death staring at them from the opposite building and were nonchalantly walking out unaware that their lives would irrevocably change after a few minutes. What transpired in the next few minutes, however, changed Dawood forever, making him invincible.

Khalid, who was extremely alert and looking around, scanning the perimeter, eyes darting like a panther after its prey, suddenly sensed the movement even before he saw the gun. He spotted the barrel of the gun, held by a man at the ground-floor window of Memnani Mansion next door. Khalid knew the man wanted Dawood first, not Khalid or Sabir. In that split second, both the gunman and Khalid acted swiftly.

The gunman pulled the trigger and a bullet flew out, whizzing towards Dawood.

'Dawood, *hato*!' Khalid screamed.

Khalid moved with amazing speed and, before the bullet could complete its trajectory, he managed to push Dawood aside and, in the same moment, whipped out his revolver hidden in the small of his back. Amirzada's bullet, which was meant for Dawood's heart, grazed Khalid's left arm. Khalid began firing at the gunman. Amirzada, who was firing at Dawood, was oblivious to Khalid and Sabir. He *had* to kill Dawood and kept firing at him. By the time he realized that Khalid had retaliated, he had already been hit below the hip and the bullet got lodged in the flesh. His crony, Alamzeb, saw the blood gushing out and realized that their game was up.

In the meanwhile, Dawood and Sabir, not ones to cower and hide, went straight for the shooter. The brothers charged towards the building, Khalid close behind them. Memnani Mansion, an old V-shaped building located at the cusp of Nagpada Junction, is renowned for the world-famous Irani hotel Sarvi, located on its ground floor. (The establishment is over ninety years old and serves the best seekh-kebab rotis in the city.)

The exchange of bullets right outside their compound alerted the Nagpada police as well, and the men rushed out to find out the source of the gunfire. Amirzada and Alamzeb, who, by now, knew they were outnumbered and outsmarted, ran for their lives.

A team of police officers yelled, *'Udhar Sarvi ke aage nikle hain, dekho'* (Look, they are running towards Sarvi).

* * *

Located in the heart of south Bombay, the Nagpada police station is in one of the most densely populated areas of the city. Perhaps it is the only police station that has quite a difficult geography as well as some interesting history. The region was earlier a predominantly Jewish locality, which explains the presence of the 157-year-old David Magen Synagogue, considered to be Asia's largest, near the Nagpada Police Hospital, as also two Jewish schools, including the E.E.E. Sassoon High School.

It is interesting to note that Gordon Hall Apartments, the high-rise building situated diagonally opposite the Nagpada police station, has an entire floor owned by Dawood's sister, and was built over the erstwhile Jewish cemetery of the Orthodox Sephardic Baghdadi Jews.

With the formation of Israel in 1948 in the Middle East, which supposedly sliced into territories of Palestine, tension was quite high among the Jews and Muslims in Bombay; this unease remained for several years until the Jews eventually migrated to Israel, Canada and other European countries. The Khilafat movement (a political movement in 1919–22 against the British move of removing the Ottomans of Turkey from the global caliphate), which traces its origin to Nagpada, had still not been forgotten by the Muslims. The locality, therefore, was a tinderbox of communal anxiety.

The area, then called the Khada Parsi, was later renamed as Nagpada Junction. The Khada Parsi, meaning 'Standing Parsi', is a huge 40-feet-tall statue of Parsi philanthropist, judge and academician Manakji Shroff. It was erected as a tribute by his youngest son, Manockjee, to immortalize his father. Seldom would a son think of such a novel way to keep the memory of his father alive. It was erected at a cost of Rs 1 lakh in 1860! Made of cast iron, it is encircled by four mermaids and boasted beautiful lights. Sadly, the lights were thieved away and, since 1970, Manakji Shroff has stood lone vigil in the dark.

Khalid was completely awestruck by the Khada Parsi landmark and often stood gazing at the statue in Nagpada, soon after his arrival in the city in 1970. Manockjee would have wanted the statue to be referred to by his father's name but 'Khada Parsi' stuck and was not easily dislodged. (Eventually, in the 1970s, traffic compulsions forced the civic body to shift the Khada Parsi statue to a spot between the two flyovers of Byculla.)

The Nagpada intersection was named after a famous Shiva temple nearby—stemming from naga, meaning 'snake', usually found garlanding Shiva's neck, while *pada* in Marathi means 'village'. In the 1980s, Nagpada Junction remained crowded for most part of the day, buzzing with people, handcart pullers and traffic until the wee hours of the night. It was easy to lose sight of someone in that crowd.

It was 1980, ten years since the statue had been shifted away to ease the congestion. The relocation was intended to impose a semblance of order on the crazy intersection. Five busy roads converged on the junction—Clare Road, Madanpura, Duncan Road, Bellasis Road and two smaller roads in Nagpada. However, the milling multitudes didn't notice any change. The handcart pullers, the famed horse-drawn Victorias, pedestrians and other vehicles continued to converge at the Nagpada Junction and proceed to stop and pause and rewind in slow motion.

* * *

Coming back to October 1980, the Pathans were now running berserk in this melee, violently shoving people aside and brandishing a gun and chopper. They knew that if they didn't escape today, it would be the last day of their lives. Just a few feet away, a furious Dawood, Sabir and Khalid were closing in on them. Occasionally the Pathans turned and fired at the chasing trio, and Khalid returned the fire from his own revolver without breaking his rapid strides. Even as these goons were chasing each other, a few uniformed cops were spiritedly following them in hot pursuit.

The bystanders watched in astonishment, perplexed. People later said that they thought they were witnessing some scene from a film shooting, and the crowd was trying to spot some film star among all the extras. After all, 1980 was the year which witnessed the maximum number of action blockbusters, including multistarrers like *Shaan, Qurbani, Dostana,* among others. It was easy to believe that what the people saw on the busy street could be an enactment of an action scene for some forthcoming movie. (Honestly, it might have been difficult for films of the time to capture such a high-octane chase sequence.) It never occurred to them that the men were actual gangsters shooting with real guns and that the underworld's gang wars had spilled on to the streets, a sign of the times to come.

An officer from the Nagpada police station later recounted that by the time they reached the turn for Alexandra Cinema, the Pathans had halted a cab, Alamzeb pushed a limping Amirzada into it, and escaped from the spot. They were terrified of Khalid, who would never have hesitated to empty his gun in to them.

Dawood and company gave chase till Cafe Andaz, an Irani joint behind Alexandra Cinema, and stopped in front of the A to Z Tailor shop. Ali Akbar Seth, the owner of the Irani hotel, and the masterji (tailor) could never forget the famous chase in their area and often recounted the whole incident with flourish. Just beyond the Irani hotel lay the brothels of Kamathipura. Dawood, Sabir and Khalid gave up the chase and walked back and met the police party, which had already stopped opposite Maharashtra College and was trying to disperse curious onlookers.

The students had come out on the road after hearing the gunfire and saw the police team and gangsters in the middle of an animated discussion, punctuated by the aggressive waving of hands and a generous use of cuss words.

The whole episode was over within a matter of minutes, but remained etched in the minds of the Nagpada residents, shopkeepers and visitors.

It was the first time that Khalid had saved Dawood's life and taken a bullet for him. Khalid's presence of mind, courage and agility had saved Dawood from certain death. This was the first such attempt from the Pathans on Dawood's life, which was only averted because of one man's daring.

Much later, people realized that Dawood owed his life to Khalid not only that day but, subsequently, on several other occasions as well. In fact, Dawood's rise to power could be pointedly attributed to Khalid. Khalid Khan, alias Khalid Pehelwan (meaning 'wrestler'), scripted Dawood's story and pushed him to do bigger things. Khalid Pehelwan made Dawood the numero uno mafia mobster of India.

2

Reel vs Real

The Rolls-Royce bearing the number plate D-1 was exempted from all traffic restrictions and regulations on the roads of Dubai. No red lights, no Dubai *shurta* (traffic police) and no rule book for the gleaming car carrying the VIP passengers.

The free-movement prerogative was something that was only reserved for Dubai's royals and eminent sheikhs of the United Arab Emirates (UAE). However, the car owner was no sheikh, not even a distant relative of the UAE's ruling families.

The car was actually gifted to Kamal Kishore Chadha by his friend of thirty-seven years, Dawood Ibrahim. The all-pervasive clout and influence of Dawood had rubbed off on Chadha in Dubai and he was considered no less influential than the don himself. Dawood's stature in Dubai, even in absentia, matched that of a royal's. Anybody associated with Dawood would, of course, share the reflected glory.

Chadha was a man of many parts and it is difficult to summarize his persona in a few words. He had been a business partner of Dawood Ibrahim's since the early 1980s. When Chadha launched his ambitious plan in the 1980s to smuggle snakeskin worth several crore rupees out of India, Dawood was his partner.

Chadha would camouflage the snakeskin in fruit baskets and smuggle them out through Kolkata. He would cross over to the Indo-Bangladesh border, going up to Dhaka and from there to London. Indian snakeskin was much valued in the European markets and commanded unheard-of prices.

Chadha was arrested once when he tried to smuggle fifty-nine cases of snakeskin in 263 boxes of fruits in a truck. The consignment was priced at Rs 44.4 lakh and intercepted at Petrapole, on the Indo-Bangladesh border. The Directorate of Revenue Intelligence (DRI) later busted the racket and arrested Chadha from his Colaba penthouse in Bombay on 19 July 1980.

Chadha was charged with being the kingpin of this smuggling racket comprising snakeskin and the skins of rare and precious reptiles. He managed to secure bail from a Bombay High Court division bench after the noted criminal lawyer Ram Jethmalani took up his case. The moniker of 'Snakeskin King' stuck to Chadha's name and that—coupled with being a partner of Dawood Ibrahim—earned him a dodgy resume in the annals of the Bombay Police.

Eventually, Chadha, being the slippery customer that he was, slithered onwards to other lucrative businesses like liquor, counterfeit currency and betting in cricket matches. To his credit, he managed to attain the stature of a kingpin in all these underhand businesses. In fact, Chadha's name figured prominently in the investigations surrounding Pakistani cricket coach Bob Woolmer's death in Kingston, Jamaica, during the 2007 Cricket World Cup.

The closed-circuit cameras of Hotel Pegasus had captured images of suspicious men, widely alleged to be Chadha and an accomplice, hastily exiting Woolmer's room after a heated exchange with the coach. Hours after the reported altercation on 18 March 2007, Woolmer's body was found in his room, strangled.

The murder caused a huge uproar because, just the day before, the Pakistani team had been disgracefully defeated by the Irish, who were then international-cricket greenhorns. Investigators alleged that both Chadha and Anis Ibrahim, Dawood's younger brother, were spotted in Jamaica. Later, Chadha's name, along with Dawood's, also cropped up in other cricket-betting scandals, including the Indian Premier League. Cricket bookie Mukesh Kochhar and his links with Dawood were widely investigated.

Beyond doubt, it is a known fact that Dawood respects Chadha far too much and addresses him as Bade Bhaiyya ('elder brother')—an agnomen that Dawood has never used for anyone since the gruesome killing of his brother Sabir in February 1981.

It was this Bade Bhaiyya of Dawood's who came to the rescue of film-maker Sanjay Gupta when his film *Shootout at Wadala* had touched a raw nerve in Dawood Ibrahim. Gupta had become a marked man for the D-Gang.

Sanjay Gupta's story is not unlike the quintessential Bollywood success story. He began by assisting film-maker Pankaj Parashar while still in his teens, and had already tasted success by the age of twenty-four. Gupta had shot to fame with his debut directorial venture, *Aatish: Feel the Fire*, starring Sanjay Dutt and Raveena Tandon.

While enjoying many successes over the years with his direction, Gupta next turned to make a sequel to 2007's *Shootout at Lokhandwala*, titled, *Shootout at Wadala*, the story of the first official police encounter involving gangster

Manya Surve. This was momentous for Gupta for many reasons. Before *Shootout at Wadala,* he had suffered a series of misfortunes, both personal and professional. Sanjay Dutt's frequent incarceration had put a spanner in the works and he had been forced to abandon plans of casting Dutt in any of his films. And then one fine day, their friendship could not withstand the pulls and pressures of the industry. Gupta's marriage also went kaput and the divorce was his personal hell for six years.

When *Shootout at Wadala* happened, things were looking up for him. He had managed to woo his wife back and married her again on the same wedding date he had married her earlier. They had a baby boy and Ekta Kapoor had promised to produce *Shootout at Wadala*. He felt happy with his life again.

Shootout at Wadala was supposed to be grander than its earlier edition. Ekta Kapoor had big plans for promoting the movie. Gupta called me for help with developing the story of the encounter for authentic details. I had already researched on Manya Surve for my book *Dongri to Dubai,* and we began to collaborate. We had long chats during the making of the movie. Gupta wanted to make an epic mafia movie and carve a niche in Bollywood for himself as the best film-maker on mafia and crime.

Gupta signed Sonu Sood and Manoj Bajpai to portray the roles of Dawood Ibrahim and Sabir Ibrahim. He had planned to use the real names behind the mafia characters in the film. Earlier, Anurag Kashyap had done this while adapting my book *Black Friday* to celluloid. His movie had received critical acclaim.

All hell, however, broke loose when Dawood and Sabir introduced themselves in the first trailer of the movie released on YouTube on 1 May 2013. Sabir was shown mercilessly butchered by his enemies, a replay of the real-life events that led to his killing.

At that point of time, the movie was almost complete, ready to be released in a few weeks. The promotions and press events were at their peak. Any movie based on a book piqued the interest of the readers. I had been lucky to have two massive book releases earlier, *Black Friday*, which was already a movie, and *Mafia Queens of Mumbai*. Vishal Bhardwaj had announced his plans to make a movie on one of the stories in the latter during its book launch. For me, the conversion of part of my third book on celluloid for the third consecutive time was a dream coming true.

My wife, Velly Thevar, was ecstatic at my personal success. She is much more talented, more creative, can write better than me and is one of the bravest women journalists I have met. Yet, at the time, she took a back seat and happily promoted my career. A vegetarian to the core, Velly threw a party for me. After years of dosas, idlis, avial and appams, she rustled up some delicious rotisserie chicken. After the dinner we both decided to conclude our celebration and call it a day.

Fifteen minutes after midnight, I received a call on my phone. The display window exhibited a Dubai number. I answered the phone and immediately recognized the voice. It was Chhota Shakeel, Dawood's man Friday. We had spoken to each other several times since I was a budding crime reporter in the *Indian Express* in the 1990s. Shakeel was livid at the apparent misrepresentation and wrong portrayal of the 'company' in the movie. He wanted the movie to be shelved. I tried to reason with him that a solution could be found for the problem. But Shakeel was furious and not willing to be hear any explanations—our conversation ended with Shakeel slamming the phone down after threatening the film's director, Sanjay Gupta, with dire consequences.

I was concerned about Gupta's safety. I knew his personal trajectory. After a turbulent personal and professional time, he had just got his bearings back. He had a little boy and his wife was expecting another baby soon. The mafia was merciless and wasted no time in carrying out their threats. For them, a living, breathing human amounted to nothing. All they know, and want, is to make a lesson out of people for others. It was 12.45 a.m., and I did not know how I could help Gupta, who had become a friend. I called him immediately but his phone was switched off.

Shakeel's tone and fury indicated that he meant business. I had tried arguing with him that it would be insane to go berserk on such a frivolous issue. I even promised him that I would give it my best shot to ensure that we try and dilute the scenes that were hurtful to Dawood and his clan.

Suddenly, I felt numb with indecision. This was becoming very serious. It was a matter of human life, stories be damned. I was reminded of the unfortunate incident of 5 August 1997. Abu Salem had told a journalist that he was going to shake up the whole film industry in a week's time. The journalist had immediately alerted the chief of the crime branch, who miscalculated and beefed up the security for film producer Pahlaj Nihalani. However, exactly a week later, on 12 August 1997, it was music magnate Gulshan Kumar who was killed.

I could never imagine visiting anyone at that unearthly hour. I was not even sure if Gupta's domestic staff would open the door for me and let me in. But I drove to his house at the far end of the city in Versova and knocked on his door. Sanjay was shocked to see Velly and me there at 1.45 in the morning.

Sanjay's anxiety hit the roof when he heard Shakeel's unholy aspirations. After *Aatish, Kaante* and *Lokhandwala,* all Sanjay wanted was another grandiose exhibition of his showmanship. Shakeel's call was threatening, to say the least. Sanjay heard me out patiently and promised to make changes to the script. We decided to change the name of the characters. That was the easiest and most sensible thing to do to pacify aggrieved minds.

But that was only the first in a series of threatening and disturbing calls that were made to me, Sanjay and others on the production team. Some film stars were threatened too. Clearly, some lives were at stake.

This was not Sanjay's first brush with the Mumbai mafia; he had had his share of run-ins with them on several occasions earlier. His first contact with them was when he was barely in his twenties, at the time of making *Ram Shastra.* Chhota Rajan had been quite miffed with him for giving a smaller or insignificant role to one of the other actors. And on other occasion he had had a longish chat with Shakeel while en route to Shirdi.

But this time it was different for Sanjay. These calls were highly menacing in tone and texture. Shakeel wanted the CDs of the movie's dialogues and scenes. Gupta, despite his reluctance, obliged and shared everything with Shakeel's messengers. Unknown to everyone, the crime branch was listening in on Shakeel's calls.

The additional commissioner of police at the time, Niket Kaushik, one of the finest police officers in the Mumbai Police, got in touch with Gupta and offered to intervene. Kaushik also offered to register a case against Shakeel and was willing to provide security, both of which Gupta refused. Kaushik also spoke to me and indicated that he was aware of the threats, and asked if I needed help. I have never thought much of police security cover and a licensed gun. Both can stymie you.

So Gupta changed the names of the main characters and the expletives were excised. Shakeel's objections were to those scenes in which Manya Surve was depicted as far more heroic than he actually was. The scenes showing Manya Surve abusing Dawood were also lopped off.

Even as Gupta was making all-out efforts to minimize the affront to the offended mafia, his troubles were far from over. On the several occasions that I met him subsequently, I realized that his trademark smile had evaporated from his face and the usual excitement and abundant energy had been replaced with fatigue and weariness. Nevertheless, Gupta was willing to take everything in his stride and plough on with his dream project.

But something happened to make Gupta lose his equilibrium and forbearance. One of the callers spoke to TV tsarina Ekta Kapoor in foul language and threatened her in an unbecoming manner. Ekta had partnered with Gupta on the project and, like him, was keen on seeing the movie released with minimum hassles. But this aggression towards Ekta was unpardonable in Gupta's eyes.

Gupta had a childhood friend by the name of Chintu Chadha, who had been arrested for a petty crime and ended up in the same cell as Iqbal Kaskar, the brother of Dawood Ibrahim, in Arthur Road Jail. The two had struck up a friendship and grown to become close. They shared tiffins, weed and other scarce luxuries. It was after Iqbal was acquitted from the Sara–Sahara case and subsequently released from jail that Chintu began worrying. He was afraid that the powerful goons in the jail would now harass and victimize him in the absence of his protector.

However, before leaving jail, Kaskar had provided an invaluable tip to Chintu, which not only saved his life but, later on, the life of his friend Sanjay as well. 'If anyone bullies you, just boast that you are the nephew of Dawood's Bade Bhaiyya, Kamal Kishore Chadha.' Chintu, who merely shared his surname with Bade Bhaiyya, had no clue who Kamal Chadha was, but he was willing to do anything to remain safe and unharmed in jail. Even before Iqbal's detractors or others could corner him, Chintu began boasting about his relationship with his famous 'uncle'. This worked like magic and none dared to cross swords with the diminutive Chintu. Chadha's name alone was enough to ensure his safety. Chintu had a peaceful stint in jail.

Gupta was aware of every aspect of this story as Chintu was his friend. On Chintu's persuasion, Gupta decided to seek help from Bade Bhaiyya. It turned out that Kamal Chadha had already heard of Gupta's increasing woes and immediately agreed to help him. Gupta had gone and met him at his plush Colaba penthouse. Chadha promised that he would not receive any more calls after that day. And to everyone's surprise, the calls actually ceased.

'Once I spoke to Mr Chadha, the incessant calls stopped. No one called me or Ekta after that. It was total peace,' Gupta recalled, sitting in the study at his Versova residence, the same place where my wife and I had gone to meet him on the night we got the first call from Chhota Shakeel.

However, Gupta could not possibly imagine the mountain of trouble and violence that had been successfully averted. It was only much later, when I began working on this book, that I realized the real danger that was lurking for him.

3

The Fall of Sabir

12 February 1981

Dawood Ibrahim was standing outside Musafir Khana on Pakmodia Street.

The street, now renamed as Husainatuz Zahra, is a Muslim cluster in south Mumbai. Like most pockets of south Mumbai's Muslim ghetto, Pakmodia Street does not have a single non-Muslim resident in the locality.

Musafir Khana (meaning 'traveller's home') served as the headquarters of Dawood's gang. Sabir and Dawood had, over a period of time, nurtured this two-storeyed structure carefully. Most of the tenants had moved out because of the fear of the Kaskar brothers and, eventually, all the dwellings in the building had come under them. Their relatives lived in some of the houses. It was the perfect place for the gang. It had a vantage view of anybody entering the colony. It also had several unoccupied rooms for visiting guests. In fact, a sizeable open area behind the building, which was located on the main road, had been encroached on by Dawood's men. If eyebrows were raised, nobody was the wiser.

The ground floor of Musafir Khana comprised Dawood's office, living rooms, godowns stacked with smuggled gold and silver bricks. In keeping with the leitmotif of his gang, there was also a torture chamber, but it was sparsely used. People buckled before Dawood's presence. For those of his victims who persisted and refused to give in, the sight of the torture chamber, dark and dreary and drab, pockmarked with bullet holes, was enough for them acquiesce. But of course the torture chamber was real and not just symbolic. Dawood's brother Sabir was a tough cookie and had no qualms about using it sometimes. On the contrary, his brother Dawood did not feel the need to use the chamber as often; he inspired a lot of awe and respect, and had a way with people. There was something about Dawood—he managed to sweet-talk his opponent into submission. While Sabir was seen as more of a goon, Dawood seemed, surprisingly, to have a heart. He inspired loyalty.

Dawood loved Musafir Khana. It was his personal fiefdom, his accomplishment. It represented what he was. He would have loved to live there and die there. He felt at home in Musafir Khana, surrounded by his loved ones and close associates and, of course, his wealth. The place made him strong and powerful, and invincible, almost.

On that particular day, on account of the lazy biorhythmic cycle that he had got into—sleeping late and waking up around noon—he had a very late dinner and, after some chitchat, went out for a post-supper stroll. His chest felt very heavy and he wondered if he had indigestion. He was uneasy, and that was unusual for him. It was around 2 a.m. and he was standing outside the massive wrought-iron gate of Musafir Khana.

He was absently looking at the cylinder-shaped, red–black postbox, installed on his instructions by the post office, right outside the gates of Musafir Khana. Not many would know that this postbox was supposed to be installed at the intersection of Dhabbu Street and Yaqub Street, but Dawood had influenced the authorities to shift it by a few metres, so that it stood like a lone sentinel outside his gate. It was a time when the postal service was the lifeline of communication, and the postbox was always filled to the brim with letters and other documents.

One thing that Dawood had learnt early on in life was that one could get anything fixed or subverted—for a price. While the postbox outside Musafir Khana was a small postbox and a thing of convenience for the community too, there were bigger things that Dawood learnt to fix in the later stages of his life. He could manoeuvre events, engineer political upheavals, fix things in the economy, in real estate, in the film industry, in sports, in almost every sphere of life.

He handled most of this so deftly that it would appear as if things were happening organically. The Dawood nudge was not visible to anybody. A lot of whispers, yes, but nobody could prove a thing, either in big-ticket projects, infrastructure, airlines or real-estate developments. In his later life, he perfected the art of getting his detractors eliminated either by way of ratting on them or through police encounters. Again, he was not directly involved in these myriad machinations.

As the night progressed, Dawood was still in the middle of a conversation with some acolytes of his, when he noticed a speeding white wedding-flower-bedecked Ambassador car coming from the direction of Bohri Mohalla. It was unusual for the car to drive at that speed and that too '*Dawood Bhai ke area mein*'. Moreover, it was uncharacteristic for a car ferrying a bride and groom to be speeding like the wind.

Dawood was instantly alert. He had had a narrow escape from death just a few months ago, outside the Nagpada police station. But for Khalid Bhai's timely intervention, he would have been history by now. Even otherwise, since he stepped into the mafia world, he was always on guard. But since the Nagpada police-station incident he had become even more cautious and begun scanning the surroundings for suspicious activity. The car's odd movement had already put him on edge. Before he could decipher anything further about the car or its occupants, the vehicle came to a screeching halt a few feet from him and a couple of men hurriedly jumped out with guns in their hands. The temerity of the men and the guns in their hands were a dead giveaway.

Dawood realized they were planning to catch him unawares. He dashed towards the wicket gate of Musafir Khana and slammed it shut before bellowing at the top of his voice, '*Khalid Bhai, kisi ne hamla kiya hai!* (We have been attacked).'

Losing no time, Khalid, who was on the first floor, immediately leaned out of the window of his tenement with a gun, ready to shoot.

The assailants were the Pathans, of course—Amirzada, Alamzeb, Akbar Khan, Jafar Shaikh and Mamoor Khan—and they began firing indiscriminately at the walls and windows of Musafir Khana. The gang had just ambushed Sabir Kaskar at a Prabhadevi petrol pump and, after leaving him dead in his white Fiat Premier Padmini car, they decided to kill Dawood too. They immediately drove towards Dongri and decided to surprise Dawood by entering through Bohri Mohalla and not J.J. Square. It was quite likely that Dawood would have received some advance warning had they entered from the J.J. intersection.

When the Pathans saw Dawood standing outside they were jubilant and felt that since he could be caught off guard, they could liquidate him as well.

However, murderous intentions are not sufficient; the Maker's permission matters too. Dawood was seemingly destined to live longer and, once again, the Pathans' plans were thwarted by the presence of Khalid.

Like the medieval knights, or even the gladiators of Rome, who faced their adversaries by insulting them, Khalid burst out, expending all his lung power, stretching the tendons of his broad neck: '*Oye gandu . . . Idhar dekh!* (Oh, asshole . . . Look up).' And with this he opened fire at the assailants who were across the road. In military terms, Khalid had a coign of vantage over his enemies, giving him an edge over them.

Bullets sprayed like water from a fire hose from both directions. It was random and both the sides were hoping to strike lucky. The Pathans were, of course, completely gobsmacked by now. The onslaught from Musafir Khana at that time of the night was a surprise. The Pathans, known for their boorish behaviour as well as their ferociousness, were unaware that Dawood had an ace up his sleeve, who was a Pathan as well. Khalid Pehelwan was a Pathan, and no ordinary one at that. He was match for all the Pathans put together, and he was with Dawood. Before they could even formulate their next plan of action, Amirzada got hit in his ribs and his big frame crumpled to the ground.

As a bleeding Amirzada collapsed, his face down on the ground, Alamzeb and Mamoor realized that the tables had turned on them. Their woes worsened when they found that they had run out of bullets. They could not match the firepower of Khalid, who seemed to have an endless supply of bullets. The firing had only increased when Dawood also joined Khalid and began firing at his assailants from the first-floor gallery. The hail of bullets scared the Pathans further.

Presuming Amirzada had died, they decided to be selfish and save themselves. Alamzeb and Mamoor and the other henchmen got into the car, reversed sharply and drove away fast. In their hurry to escape they did not even dare or care to get Amirzada into the car. All they wanted was to leave the battlefield behind and escape a dog's death in the streets.

As soon as they left, Dawood and Khalid came down to the street and saw Amirzada bleeding. Dawood always had great foresight. He was concerned that if Amirzada died outside Musafir Khana, they would all be booked again in a murder case. Dawood wanted to avoid a murder charge at any cost, even if that meant saving the life of his enemy.

'*Bhai, agar yeh mar gaya toh hum pe 302 lag jayega aur hum phir wanted ho jayenge* (If he dies here, Section 302 [of the Indian Penal Code (IPC)] will be imposed on us and we will become "wanted" again),' said Dawood to Khalid, who was thinking hard about what to do.

Finally, Khalid said, 'No, don't worry, we can avoid this complication.'

They asked a couple of boys to dump an injured Amirzada in a cab and drop him off at the casualty ward of the J.J. Hospital, which was barely 500 metres from Musafir Khana. Thus, they managed to avoid a police investigation and legal complications.

Dawood felt victorious and relieved that he and his team had repelled the enemy attack even in spite of being unprepared and caught unawares. He was also happy that they had almost managed to kill his arch-enemy Amirzada.

Dawood's euphoria was short-lived. He had underestimated the Pathans. While he survived that night, his brother Sabir was not so lucky. That night, the Pathans had wanted to kill two birds with one stone. Dawood survived but Sabir succumbed. At the same J.J. Hospital where Amirzada had been admitted, Sabir was wheeled in a gurney, his body soaked in blood. His body looked mauled. He had been killed at a Prabhadevi petrol pump while on a rendezvous with his girlfriend from the Congress House brothel in Kamathipura. J.J. Hospital informed the Mumbai Police who, in turn, arrested the injured Amirzada for the crime.

Dawood did not know about Sabir's death until it was too late. He was shattered to the core when he saw his brother's limp, lifeless body lying mutilated and butchered on the stretcher outside the casualty ward of J.J. Hospital. Dawood's men had never seen him crying earlier. He was their tough boss who never exhibited his emotions in public. But that night they saw him bawling like a baby. Sabir's funeral was a grand one in keeping with his status as Dawood's brother, and as the boss of the gang; as Sabir was older to him, Dawood had always liked his elder brother to believe that he was in charge.

Sabir was buried in Bada Kabristan in Nariyalwadi, Marine Lines. It was attended by most residents of Bohri Mohalla, lest their absence was noticed. Among Muslims, one's presence in a funeral is an expression of solidarity in a time of grief and mourning, and skipping it is believed to reveal the rancour held against the dead and their mourners.

In the 1980s, Bal Thackeray, head of the regional political party Shiv Sena, decided to pursue his political ambitions by using local Maharashtrians to protest on most issues. So, if he called a bandh, the entire city would shut shop fearing the wrath of Shiv Sena's cadres. The only place where the bandh was ineffective was Bohri Mohalla. The Shiv Sainiks didn't dare to step into this Muslim bastion. The Shiv Sena and the Muslims of Mumbai hated each other.

But on the day that Sabir was buried, every shop in the business district of the Muslim ghetto, right from the Crawford Market stretch to Byculla, was closed. There were muffled whispers in street corners, '*Sabir shaheed ho gaya* (Sabir has been martyred),' '*Sabir ka inteqaal ho gaya* (Sabir is dead).'

Nevertheless, that night was a game changer for the Mumbai mafia in so many ways. It marked the commencement of gruesome violence in the city. A brother had been killed and a house attacked. After these blatant violations of the unwritten codes of the Mumbai underworld had been committed, nothing was sacrosanct any more.

Dawood took charge of the gang and, since the Pathans were now regarded as his arch-enemies, he swore to decimate any Pathan who dared cross his path.

There was one small footnote, however, that everyone missed in the mayhem. It was a Pathan who had saved Dawood's life from the other Pathans. Twice in Dawood's life a Pathan had put himself at grave risk to defend a young man in the throes of notorious fame.

In the mafia, it is a given that one always lays one's life on the line. But it is an unwritten rule that the ones who live are actually the ones who are smart and lucky enough to have not been foolish. Sacrifices are alien and non-existent. One man, however, defied the odds to not save his life but that of his protégé.

Dawood owed his life and power to this man.

The story of this Pathan—Khalid Khan, alias Khalid Pehelwan, alias KP—was untold yet.

4

The First Lead

Among the various threats that film-maker Sanjay Gupta received from the many ganglords, one of them was from Khalid Khan, or Khalid Pehelwan.

The revelation was stunning for me. I had presumed that the gangsters of yore had, by now, hung up their boots. Since I knew that Khalid was not in India, nor Pakistan, I thought he had died a rich man in some European city. But the caller who threatened Sanjay Gupta was clearly menacing and warned him of life-threatening consequences if there was any misrepresentation of his character in the movie *Shootout at Wadala*. This seemed to bear the mark of the underworld.

I had always been keen on profiling Khalid while working as a crime reporter at *Indian Express* and later at *Mid-Day*. However, despite my best efforts to track down his family and relatives or his aides, I had been unable to make much headway.

In my limited understanding of the Mumbai mafia, I had always felt that Khalid was an unlikely gangster and did not belong to the oligarchy of Dawood's gang. Yet, he had become integral to the growing clout, notoriety and power of the gang.

Had it not been for him, Dawood would not have been Dawood. He would have perished in obscurity long ago, killed either by his rivals or the police. Khalid Pehelwan always came in the way, making Dawood invincible.

It is always easier to track down and speak to an active don whose lieutenants are positioned all over the city, as some of the police officers may be in touch with them. But how does one track down a ganglord who has retired and is untraceable.

It was an arduous and challenging task but not impossible. Khalid Khan was a Pathan, and quite well known in their circles. But the Pathans were wary of me because I had written about Dawood. Dawood's story is so much about how he vanquished the Pathans.

My hunt for a lead for the Khalid Pehelwan story was tiring and exhaustive. I tracked down virtually all of Madanpura, Byculla, Baida Gully near Novelty Cinema and other localities in south Mumbai that housed clusters of Pathan residences.

I was completely focused on finding Khalid. My routine comprised making several calls a day, knocking on scores of doors in a week and being discreet about my search for an erstwhile Pathan ganglord. I also sought out journalists to check with their own sources if they could obtain Khalid's whereabouts.

One vital piece of intelligence that I managed to gather from various quarters was that Khalid might have relatives in Ahmedabad and that I could find them in the Kalupura area of the city. Mumbai was my bailiwick, but Ahmedabad would be difficult since there are a lot of Pathan settlements there. The Pathans, when they first set foot in India six centuries earlier, had taken a particular liking for Gujarat.

Mumbai Pathans are distinguishable due to their distinct features. They are tall, well built and extremely fair, with curly red hair, and speak accented Urdu or Hindi. Many Gujarati Pathans, on the other hand, are so assimilated into the regional culture that it is difficult to distinguish them from other Muslims; for instance, the famous Pathan brothers of Indian cricket, Yusuf and Irfan Pathan.

I was a bit disheartened at the prospect of pounding the streets of Ahmedabad and almost contemplated giving up on Khalid. But out of the blue I got a call. It seemed as if all my persistence had paid off. A stroke of good fortune got me the contact I was desperately looking for. Most of the stories I have written about in newspapers, or even in my books, have come about due to sheer luck. And so was the case this time as well.

It was an unknown number; I was wary of answering it. In my line of work unsaved numbers are not a good omen. But as a father of two reckless and accident-prone teenage sons, I didn't want to ignore such calls for unspeakable reasons.

The voice on the other end was gruff, but I could discern the recognizable Pathani accent. The man was warm and courteous and said that he wanted to meet me. My hopes soared and I cancelled all my assignments and rushed over.

Our first meeting was near Maratha Mandir Cinema in Mumbai Central. The man I met was in his late forties, very red and fair like a Parsi; he had a thick red moustache and sported a Muslim fez cap. He seemed to trust me, and I liked his goofy manner.

He introduced himself as Sayed Sikandar Shah. He turned out to be not only the top confidant of Khalid Khan but his relative by marriage too. Sikandar himself had been named in several cases, including an assault case along with the Pathan patriarch and don Karim Khan, alias Karim Lala.

Sikandar had spent over seven years in jail for smuggling and extortion cases. In Arthur Road Jail, his cellmate was the top dog drug lord Nari Khan, Mumbai's most notorious drug baron and an ally of gangster Amar Naik. Both Nari Khan and Amar Naik had been killed in a police encounters, at the hands of Inspector Vasant Dhoble and Inspector Vijay Salaskar, respectively.

At one point of time, when the Mumbai Police was trigger-happy, Sikandar Shah had been on the hit list of an encounter-specialist cop. In fact, he had also arrested Sikandar with 2 kg cocaine once. Sikandar knew that unless he did something desperately smart, his days were numbered.

When Sikandar Shah learnt—through his snitch in the police department—that his dossier was being prepared, he felt a knot tightening in his stomach. He was involved with the mafia but that was not reason enough for him to be bumped off. He had not murdered anybody and neither was he a threat to anybody. He had a family; his children were toddlers.

After a lot of thinking, Sikandar developed a clear strategy. He decided to use the law against the law and the police against the police. It is a dangerous game and has often misfired badly on people who attempted this. But Sikandar turned out to be among the lucky few.

He decided to surrender to the neighbouring state police. Since he already had a base in Gujarat, he decided to surrender to a police station in Porbandar. One day he simply walked into a police station, declaring, 'I am wanted in several cases in Mumbai and would like to surrender voluntarily so that I get leniency from the courts.'

For the Gujarat Police, this was a prize catch. A wanted and absconding criminal had been netted without much trouble. They happily arrested him and, for good measure, subjected him to torture for a couple of days to get more information out of him. But Sikandar knew how much to reveal and when to keep the lid closed tight. Finally, the police contacted their counterparts in the Mumbai Police's Anti-Narcotics Cell and asked them to take his custody.

And so fate decreed that Sikandar survived the encounter specialist.

Sikandar was produced before the sessions court judge J.W. Singh on 4 November 1995. The police wanted only a one-day remand but Judge Singh gave him six-days' remand. The narcotics cell did not have a lock-up to keep Sikandar in for six days. So the police moved around with him across the town for six days in their police jeep. No other criminal in the country would have been so lucky to have received such a detention—moving around town in an air-conditioned police vehicle, breaking bread with the policemen and sleeping comfortably through it all, knowing full well that he could not be bumped off, even by accident, because the court was watching.

Subsequently, Sikandar was remanded to judicial custody and sent to Arthur Road Jail. He spent seven years in jail with several top criminals and drug peddlers—Santosh Shetty, Sadhu Shetty and Bharat Nepali were his cellmates. But he was happiest to meet one particular accused towards the end of his jail tenure.

In a strange twist, on 20 March 2000, Judge Singh, who had sentenced Sikandar, was arrested by the Mumbai police for collusion with Chhota Shakeel. Singh was alleged to have hired Shakeel to recover Rs 40 lakh from a businessman in Mumbai and, in return, he had agreed to acquit two aides of Shakeel involved in serious offences. The Mumbai Police had tapped the conversation between Judge Singh and Shakeel and their intermediary advocate, Liyaqat Ali Shaikh. Subsequently, the sessions court trial judge was slapped with provisions of the Maharashtra Control of Organized Crime Act and sent to jail.

Sikandar spent hours talking to the judge, who claimed he had been framed by the police. Sikandar spent over a couple of years in jail with the judge until he was released on 11 October 2002.

Once out of jail, Sikandar had learnt more tricks and brushed up on his skills to dodge the law. Indian jails, like most all over the world, do not reform criminals. They harden the criminals and incentivize their foray in crime. So, seven years later, the Sikandar Shah that emerged was none the wiser for his incarceration. Instead, he now knew his raison d'être—hawala and kidnapping for ransom. (The system detested murderers and drug peddlers.)

By now, Sikandar had the temerity to kidnap a whole gang of fifteen people at once—an unimaginable feat even for the *bahubalis* (strongmen) of Bihar or the kidnapping mafia of Uttar Pradesh.

In a hawala transaction, one Miyaji* of Bharuch, a well-known history-sheeter, had siphoned off over 4000 Kuwaiti rials (equivalent to Rs 5 lakh), which he was supposed to pay to Sikandar in Mumbai. So when Sikandar, along with a few bouncers, visited Miyaji's office in Bharuch, Miyaji had taken the precaution of surrounding himself with fifteen of his men. Sikandar demanded his money from Miyaji but the cunning racketeer feigned ignorance of any such transaction. Sikandar was half-prepared for this eventuality. His men immediately shoved their guns in Miyaji's face. His army of men were stunned at so many guns and Miyaji being held captive at gunpoint.

---

* Name changed.

Since leaving any eyewitness on the spot would have compounded his troubles, Sikandar threatened everyone and piled up all fifteen men in two waiting Ambassador cars. Sikandar had removed all the door-opening handles and glass sliders, so neither could the car doors be opened from inside nor the glasses rolled down. The overloaded cars chugged to Mumbai and the men were packed like sardines, but they could not escape.

The men were forcibly checked into a seedy joint in Mumbai. The gunmen monitored each and every movement of these men, including their meals and ablutions. One man even accompanied them to the toilets. They were kept cooped up until Miyaji made a call to his men and organized the money he owed to Sikandar.

When Miyaji and his team returned to Bharuch, they were embarrassed. The news of the incident and the way Sikandar had engineered it had spread far and wide. This also reached the ears of Fazlur Rehman, a notorious criminal and kidnapping kingpin involved in several kidnappings in Ahmedabad and Delhi, including that of the Adani Group chairman, Gautam Adani. Adani was released only after a ransom of Rs 15 crore was paid. Fazlur happened to be placed in Sabarmati Central Jail, Ahmedabad, during the trial of the Adani case, and he was surprised at this kidnapping incident and wanted to look into Sikandar's antecedents.

Fazlur began making inquiries about Sikandar and was totally taken aback by what he uncovered: that Sikandar was a relative of Khalid's and that Fazlur should not mess with him.

After a couple of meetings I realized that Sikandar was a devout Muslim who never missed a namaz, often making me wait on the road because it was time for one of the five mandatory prayers for the day. I remained a sport throughout these long waiting sessions. He made up for it by treating me to gallons of fresh carrot juice.

Sikandar was a Bollywood buff and held Dilip Kumar and Kader Khan in high esteem. In fact, he loved all the Khans of the film industry, and had actually had a few cameos in a couple of movies.

After several meetings in between the namaz timings, I decided to disclose the reasons for meeting him. Sikandar promised to set up a meeting with Khalid but remained vague, until one day he agreed to make me talk to him on the phone.

We met at Queen Mary Hotel near Ismailia Hospital in Byculla and, somehow, the conversation steered towards *Shootout at Wadala*. Sikandar's face reddened with fury. He seemed to be visibly upset at Sanjay Gupta for his rash portrayal of Khalid Pehelwan in the movie and was itching to take punitive measures against the film-maker.

'Sanjay Gupta's office was located near an intersection. These were MHADA row houses converted into offices. We conducted a recce of his office and planned to attack him if he misbehaved with Khalid Bhai.'

Sikandar recounted how Gupta could have staved off the threat from Dawood's gang but he did not even know that he was also on the radar of Khalid Pehelwan's team. Gupta apparently had to placate Khalid Pehelwan and convince him that there was nothing offensive about his portrayal in the movie. Khalid was finally convinced, but not Sikandar Shah.

'*Bhai ne mana kar diya, nahin toh hum log full tayyari mein the* (Bhai said no, otherwise we were fully prepared),' he said casually over gallons of carrot juice.

In my twenty years of crime journalism I had heard about Khalid Pehelwan plenty of times. I heard that the man had retired from mafia chieftainship and was now a recluse. So it was interesting to see how one movie created so much sensation that Khalid was forced out of his self-imposed isolation.

As we were busy talking, Sikandar's phone rang suddenly. I was surprised to see that the man who, until moments ago was the picture of authority and power, was now the embodiment of humility.

'*Jee, Bhai . . . Jee, Bhai . . . Jee, Bhai . . . Mere saamne baithe hain* (Yes, Bhai . . . He is sitting in front of me).'

Then he passed his old and outdated Nokia phone to me.

'*Salaam alaikum, main Khalid bol raha hoon* (Salaam alaikum, this is Khalid speaking),' were the first words he uttered.

'*Jee, farmaiyye* (Yes, please tell me).'

He began by mentioning my book *Dongri to Dubai* and immediately expressed his resentment over the way I had described him in the book. Khalid was particularly upset over a scene in the book where I had depicted the push-up competition between him and his former boss Bashu Dada, in which he had lost to Bashu.

'I want to clarify that I could never lose to Bashu and that you got your facts wrong.'

Khalid ranted for a while and then the phone got cut. I was not sure if he had slammed the phone down or whether it was a call drop.

I had to meet Khalid. I wanted his side of the story. I had always wanted to meet Dawood's mentor. I also wanted to know the motivations that drove a *pehelwan* (wrestler) into the mafia's waiting arms. And most of all I was interested in knowing how Khalid Pehelwan survived Dawood's ire. Imagine disassociating with Dawood and living to tell the tale. I wanted to know why Dawood respected his mentor.

That evening at the Queen Mary Hotel with Sikandar Shah was very fruitful. I was already making plans to travel to Dubai once again to meet Khalid Khan.

5

The Dubai Rendezvous

The few seconds seemed to stretch on for eternity when Rayyan, my protégé, remained suspended in mid-air, poised like Superman with his arms outstretched. At twenty-eight, Rayyan weighed in at a solid 90 kg, had a squat built and was muscular. But the man who hoisted him over his shoulders, much like a WWF wrestler would, was a seventy-year-old. When Rayyan finished his Superman pose and was back on terra firma, his head was spinning. But the man who swung him up like a rag doll didn't lose any sweat. Leave alone panting or any signs of exertion, the elderly Khalid Pehelwan didn't even register an increased heartbeat. Khalid was demonstrating his physical prowess by lifting Rayyan in this elegant five-star-hotel room. For years, after reading *Dongri to Dubai,* he had been angry with me for mentioning his lack of strength vis-à-vis Bashu Dada. And now he was a cocking a snook at me. I apologized and ate humble pie.

'*Tumne meri taaqat ka namuna dekh liya* (I hope you have got some idea about my strength now),' he said with a triumphant smile. Khalid is almost 6 feet 2 inches, hair dyed jet black, with a receding hairline, a thick moustache and a firm jaw. He looks like an extremely fit man in his early sixties. Donning a beige suit, he looked dapper in his hotel room overlooking the beautiful Dubai harbour.

The view outside was simply not Dubaiesque. With glass and chrome buildings, the city has long since left behind its former 'arid desert' image. But here in this part of Dubai there is organization, of course, but there are also dhows and boats anchored cheek by jowl, constantly offloaded with all kinds of goods. It looked like a scene straight out of an Indiana Jones movie—the bazaar, the goods, the colours. While across the harbour you could see the skyline of modern-day Dubai, below the hotel it was like Gateway of India. There was a lot of chaos but the shimmering blue water and the view was simply spectacular.

While pressing Khalid for this meeting, I got the impression that he was not very keen on the same. He had his apprehensions about meeting a writer. He thought I was a snooping journalist out to expose him for a television scoop.

Soon after I had spoken to him from Sikandar's phone in Mumbai, I decided to meet Khalid in Dubai. I landed in Dubai on 9 February 2017. I had no idea that I was being followed from the airport by an unmarked car—I remained totally oblivious to my shadow. These are lessons in humility for me. I had always claimed that I could spot any car tailing me after three signals. But this time I had been caught unawares.

Dubai was no longer as energetic and vibrant as I found it to be during my last visit, when I had managed to track down Abu Salem's top confidant, childhood friend and cousin, Abu Kalam, in 2014. Abu Kalam had revealed to me absolutely unknown details about Salem's life, which had even astonished Salem when he read my book. He was curious to know the source. But there were several. And though Abu Kalam only told me about Salem's personal life, I didn't reveal his identity. Abu Kalam is now dead, of course, having succumbed to some illness.

During my 2017 visit, I saw a changed Dubai. While things looked the same on the surface, the malls pulsing with a thousand nationalities, the global recession had definitely left its imprint. While there still seemed to be a lot of construction activities, I was told there had been a slump in real estate and other businesses—over 300 small businesses that were flourishing shut down without notices and business owners reported bankruptcy.

The don who had kick-started his journey as a billionaire from the soil of Dubai—linking his fortunes with that of a growing city from the 1980s to the mid 1990s—was himself a victim of the recession. Dawood Ibrahim had partnered with many local sheikhs in the UAE with business investments worth over Rs 3500 crore in Dubai. The economic downturn was also making him bleed, mainly due to the change in exchange rates, which, in turn, affects hawala rates. As I sauntered through the streets and malls I could sense a feeling of gloom and stoicism. Dubai's massive workforce boasts over 40 lakh Indians, mostly from Kerala, which results in making the Indian government richer through an annual remittance of USD 10 billion, figures released by the state government of Kerala.

Rayyan had left after checking me into a nondescript apartment hotel near Deira. The man had to struggle for a living, the country was not as sparkling with opportunities as it was until a couple of years ago. That night I received a call from a Dubai number asking me to be at the coffee shop of the Hyatt Regency hotel at noon. I was restless through the night and, consequently, did not feel my best in the morning.

As I was being escorted to the meeting, I recalled my first disastrous meeting with Khalid Pehelwan. It happened in a room reeking of opulence, affluence and power. Two suits were standing outside the door. We had started off well after we shook hands. He seemed courteous. But my laptop bag came in the way. His perception of journalists in Mumbai was limited to a khadi-kurta-clad person with a *jhola* (cloth bag)—the image reinforced by movies in the 1970s. I, on the contrary, had burst on to the journalism scene in 1995, when the khadi and the jhola were on the wane. By the turn of the new century, journalists had transitioned from pagers to the massive handset-mobile phones that looked like walkie-talkies. And by the time 2010 rolled around, it was common for journalists to look like corporate honchos with laptop bags in tow.

Khalid instantly took a dislike to my laptop and got very upset. Perhaps he had seen too much *sansanikhez khabar* (the so-called 'sensational scoops') on television and presumed that I was there to do a sting on him. After a brief debate, he insisted that the laptop bag be kept outside the room as he was not sure if I would record our conversation on the sly and, therefore, the bag was thrown on the sofa in the corridor. We spoke briefly for half an hour. But his hostile attitude seemed to suggest that he thought I was carrying a hidden camera on my person. He graciously offered me a strongly brewed tea laced with honey, served by a liveried waiter. The laptop bag had set the tone for the meeting and we didn't cover much ground.

I was jolted back to the present time as the lift opened into the corridor and I was ushered into the hotel room. I kept my fingers crossed, hoping Khalid would find no reason to stall the interview this time. After last time's laptop fiasco I had had to wait in Dubai for days, hoping Khalid would call. Finally, I gave up and left for Mumbai. That was over two years ago.

In fact, this time I told him that I had company. I was asking Rayyan Rizvi to tag along to take notes. Rayyan's dad and I go back a long way. I was part of Rayyan's growing-up years and knew that he harboured aspirations to become a sports journalist. He was a good observer and had even worked under me as a sports reporter while I helmed *Asian Age* in Mumbai. He now lives in Dubai with his wife and children and is engaged in the export–import business.

Before the meeting, Khalid had asked me to wait outside the Salah Al Din metro station at 5 p.m. A black SUV came by, and the burly driver, who recognized me from a distance, waved at me to get inside the car. I was a bit frazzled at being recognized so clearly by a stranger. Was he shown photographs of me, or did he google my images? Was it safe? Will a sniper be setting his lenses on me now? I was plagued by insecurities.

However, pushing away negative thoughts, Rayyan and I got inside the car. I made an effort to make small talk but the driver was seemingly well-trained in the art of verbal warfare—he remained polite throughout and only replied with a 'jee' (yes) as the standard answer to all my questions. The conversation went something like this:

'Is Dubai as chaotic as Mumbai?'

'Jee.'

'What do you do for Khalid Bhai?'

'Jee.'

'For how many years have you been working for him?'

'Jee.'

'Are you Indian or Pakistani?'

'Jee.'

It was as if he had been robotically programmed not to deviate from his set replies. I gave up.

The vehicle made a sharp turn and entered a building basement, which was more like a dark cavern-like alley, reminding me of a scene from Kamal Haasan's disastrous spy flick *Vishwaroopam*. We were taken through a secret entry point and straight into a parking lot. A special lift took us straight to Khalid's office. I had no idea where we were, but I had learnt my lesson early in life—not to ask too many questions.

Khalid was quite welcoming this time and, to my surprise, he was quite charming with Rayyan as well.

'Tumhara *bhatija* (Your nephew)?'

I nodded vigorously.

'Your features match with his, it's a dead giveaway,' he said, trying to be charming.

I had tried to be cautious this time and had left my laptop bag behind. Khalid ordered a nice meal for us and served us equally refreshing tea with honey. Dubai's hotels cannot satisfy one with good Indian tea; although Pakistani establishments like the Raavi chain of hotels do make a good brew, they often dilute how crisp the tea is with too much sugar.

Khalid was in a much more candid mood today and quite forthcoming. It was during the course of the conversation that I asked him about how he had ended up conjoining his name with the title of a wrestler. In the Mumbai underworld there are many titles used to address gangsters, but most of them are pejoratives—Salim Kutta (dog), Iqbal Mirchi (chilli), Anil Wangya (brinjal), Umar Dhakkan (dick-headed), and so on. But Khalid had managed to receive a unique title. A pehelwan is not just a healthy man or a wrestler but a man with a massive physique.

Khalid responded to my pehelwan question with full-throated laughter. I was reminded of Amjad Khan's portrayal of Gabbar Singh in *Sholay*.

It was then that he told me his story, about how he grew up to be a wrestler, defeating opponents in a jiffy and winning national-level trophies, including the Bharat Kumar (a freestyle wrestling competition organized by the Haryana government). He related that he had inherited his wrestling skills as a hand-me-down from his father who was also a wrestler. His father had taught him the tricks of the trade and the magic formula to defeat the strongest of opponents.

I was, at first, sceptical of Khalid's claims of invincibility. It was then that he got up from behind the table and asked Rayyan to step forward. And before the bewildered boy knew it, he was being help high up in the air.

I was given a first-hand demonstration of the former wrestler's stunning physical prowess—additionally impressive considering he was well past his prime, by at least four decades. I have spent enough time in the gym to know what it takes to command that kind of strength.

After Rayyan's airlift, it seemed like the ice broke and the conversation suddenly became more animated and exciting, and since Khalid was in a forthcoming and generous mood, I decided to make this count and get my queries answered. He spoke of how, in his college days, he had been challenged to a fight and how, in a stunning upset, he had knocked out his rival. And then there was no looking back.

This turned out to be an endless meeting, with countless cups of tea.

Khalid's story was a fascinating saga of a bright student who not only ended up with the Mumbai mafia but graduated to becoming the mentor of a powerful don like Dawood Ibrahim.

6

The Legend of Pathans

Since Bollywood serves as our ready reckoner for what different kinds of people and tribes are supposed to look like, and tragicomically also shapes our perceptions about communities, who could better embody the mighty race of the Pathans than the stalwart of Hindi cinema, the one and only Amitabh Bachchan. Remember *Khuda Gawah*—with kohl-lined eyes, Bachchan swept us into the world of the Pathans, their fierce loyalty, their sense of honour, the sense of pride in their clan. Like the Rajputs of India, their community is bound by an unwritten code, where honour is paramount, where their word is their bond even if they have to sacrifice all that they hold dear in life.

So we see Pran's Sher Khan in *Zanjeer*, Shah Rukh Khan in *Hey Ram* and Salman Khan in *Sanam Bewafa*, all of them showcasing a Pathan. The nationalist freedom fighter Khan Abdul Gaffar Khan, known as Frontier Gandhi, crystallized in our heads the image of a Pathan as a benevolent, soft person with a big heart, in a big frame.

The Pathans have their own take on their history and antecedents: King Talut, known as King Saul in the Old Testament, had left behind an orphaned grandson by the name of Afghana, who was brought up by Hazrat Dawood, or David, as his own son. Afghana grew up with Solomon, who later anointed him 'Malak Afghana' and made him the commander in chief of his massive army; Afghana eventually helped in the construction of Masjid Al-Aqsa in Jerusalem. His multiple conquests took him to an area bordering Russia, which is now in present-day Afghanistan; he died here and was buried near the Sulaiman mountains near Zhob.

Thousands of years later, when the Prophet of Islam, Hazrat Muhammad, gave a clarion call and invited the world towards Islam, the message reached far and wide. The tribes near Zhob and the regions of Ghor were also eager to meet him and investigate the truth of the Prophet. All the tribes got together and deputed a noble scholarly man, Pehtan Qais, to visit the Holy Prophet in Mecca to gather more facts about this new religion. Qais undertook an arduous journey to Mecca. After his meeting with Prophet Muhammad he embraced Islam. Legend has it that Qais was renamed as Qais Abdur Rashid by the Prophet himself. One of the companions of the Prophet, Khalid bin Waleed, had his daughter betrothed to Qais, who returned to his country and disseminated the religion further.

Since the Zhobi tribals spoke Pashtun and were known as the Pehtan, it was difficult for the Arabs to pronounce it. The Arabic language does not have the sound for *pa* in its repertoire, so Pakistan becomes 'Bakistan' for an Arab. Pehtan became 'Bataan', which was further corrupted to 'Pathan'. Since Afghanistan was also a trade border, with Iran close by, the Arabs began exploiting their martial instincts and roped in the Pathans as part of the armies for several conquests where they used violence to spread Islam. After the demise of Prophet Muhammad, the successive caliphs used the might of the Pathans to spread Islam in countries like Iran and Syria. The Syrian army was defeated with the assistance of Pathans, who were related to Khalid bin Waleed. It is said that the Pathans were thus instrumental in the spread of Islam to western Asia within the first fifty years of its advent. Ghazni, Ghour and seventy-six other tribal areas had converted to Islam. It is a different story that the Ghaznis and Ghouris unleashed an untold tale of violence, bloodshed, tyranny and plundering in India, which, to this day, has discoloured the glory of Islam for generations of Indians.

Coming back to Qais (who was the thirty-seventh descendant of King Saul), he specified in his will that he should be buried close to the Takht-e-Sulaiman, or the grave of Malak Afghana, in the Baluchistan region near the Federally Administered Tribal Areas (or FATA) of Pakistan. The Pathans are proud to state that they have origins in Pakistan and not Afghanistan. They also proudly trace their lineage to Malak Afghana and Qais Abdur Rashid, the legendary aide to the Holy Prophet.

However, in the pre-Independence era, the region had limited opportunities for economic growth and even the generation of income. Agriculture was the main occupation but it was not enough to sustain large families. This spurred the exodus of Pathans to more prosperous places in India like Mumbai, Gujarat and Bhopal.

History records that the Pathans arrived in India in batches, as armies of various rulers. The earliest settlement dates back to the time when Mahmud of Ghazni invaded Gujarat in 1024 AD. They were also part of Muhammad Bin Tughlak's army in the 14th century. Then another batch arrived during the rule of Mahmud Begada. After the end of the Mughal era, the Pathans rose to become rulers of the princely states of Gujarat like Junagadh and Palanpur. Gujarat has an assortment of Pathans. There are the Babai, or Babi Pashtun tribe, and the Jalori Pathans. Yesteryears actress Parveen Babi is a descendent of the Junagadh Pashtun rulers. The Babi dynasty also ruled Balasinor (Vadasinor) in Kheda district. In the later years, towards the 19th century, more Pashtuns arrived from Afghanistan and settled in Ahmedabad, Surat, Khambat and even Mumbai. Most of the Pathans of Gujarat were rulers of the princely states of Gujarat like Palanpur, Junagadh, Balasinor and Radhanpur.

Most of the Pathans who migrated to northern India hailed from Batkhela, in the Malakand district of Khyber Pakhtunkhwa in Pakistan. It was a breathtakingly beautiful place. Legend has it that Batkhela has existed since the time of King Ashoka. The chieftain who ruled the region was called Butt, and the township was named after him as Battkheda. The place is in the Swat region and is now pronounced as 'Baathkhela'. Abdur Raheem Bacha, also known as Raheem Khan in those days, moved to Bhopal in India at the turn of the century, like many of his ancestors, in search of a better life.

Bhopal was one of the cities that the Pathans had a great affinity for. The city was established in 1724 by the Afghan Sardar Dost Mohammed Khan, who was a commander in the Mughal army. When the Mughal empire was on the wane, the commander usurped Mangalgarh and Bherasia, the latter is now a tehsil of Bhopal. His story illustrates how the legend of Pathan honour took root over centuries. When Khan's nephew assassinated the Gond queen Kamalapati's husband, he executed his own nephew and returned the queen's kingdom back to her. The queen was very impressed and gave him a huge sum of money and a village. It is another story that after the death of the last Gond queen, Khan seized the kingdom and established a capital called Islampur, 10 km from modern-day Bhopal. His successors, who by then were independent of the Mughal rulers, took on the title of 'Nawab' and declared Bhopal an independent state. The Hindu Marathas seized control of the neighbouring states but Bhopal remained elusive under the Pashtun nawabs and begums because they had stood with the British in all the three Anglo-Maratha wars and also the 1857 mutiny. They were loyal to the British always and were the last to sign the Instrument of Accession to India on 1 May 1949, handing over the state of Bhopal to India.

Nawab Hamidullah Khan of the Harda and Bhopal provinces was the heir to the throne of Bhopal and Harda. (The nawab is the maternal grandfather of cricketer Mansoor Ali Khan Pataudi (actor Saif Ali Khan's father). Raheem Khan went to see Nawab Hamidullah Khan, who instantly took a liking to him and made him his personal bodyguard. They shared a great bond which grew over the years. After Nawab Hamidullah Khan officially succeeded his mother, Sultan Kaikhusrau Jehan Begum, in 1926, Raheem became the chief commander of the nawab's forces. Raheem was solely devoted to the nawab. He did not have a large family like other Pathans. Raheem's wife, Mehrunissa, and two children, Yusuf and Shahnaz, comprised his little world. Since he did not have the time to take care of his family, his childless brother-in-law Shaikh Afzal took the children under his wing.

This was a turning point in young Yusuf Khan's life, which also set the course for the future generations. Shaikh Afzal, Yusuf's maternal uncle, was an aspiring wrestler and so began training the boy in wrestling. Those were the days when the legend of Mian Ghulam Muhammad Pehelwan, better known as 'Gama Pehelwan', had taken the country by storm. Hailed as the Indian Hercules, his unbeatable strength and courage in the ring were renowned around the whole country. During his visit to England in the 1930s, Gama had knocked down thirty Japanese wrestlers in an hour and humiliated the Polish phenomenon Stanislaus Zbyszko, who escaped from the fight after he saw Gama's tenacity and strength. It is said that even Bruce Lee was inspired by Gama.

It turned out that the legend of Gama had inspired millions of youths in the country. Every Muslim youth wanted to become Gama in those days. Yusuf Khan's ancestral profession was farming but he was fired up with aspirations of becoming another Gama in the wrestling arena. In turn, Shaikh Afzal, Yusuf's adoptive father, wanted to fulfil his own dreams of becoming another Gama, through Yusuf. However, Yusuf could not fulfil his lifelong aspirations and passed on the dream to his progeny.

Yusuf had five sons: Shetaab, Yaqoob, Khalil, Khalid and Habib. Yusuf got all of them into the wrestling ring. Yusuf's passion for wrestling was such that he could forgive his sons' neglect of their studies but he could never overlook their laxity in the gymnasium. All five brothers had strict daily routines and diets chalked out by their father. Their day began at the crack of dawn with 100 *dand baithaks*, the Indian version of the American squat. The American squat involved placing a heavy barbell on the shoulder and doing several sets until failure for muscle hypertrophy. However, the Indian squats were closer to the Bulgarian regime, or what is now known to the contemporary world as German Volume Training (or GVT), which is several sets of tens till failure.

After this the boys would follow with over 100 push-ups or dips, which is known as 'surya namaskar' among Indian wrestlers. This regimen primed all the muscles in both the lower and upper body. All the five boys would unfailingly, unflinchingly and unswervingly devote themselves to developing their bodies. The idea was to get broader and have more muscles.

The 56-inch-chest refrain that Prime Minister Narendra Modi is heard throwing at his detractors is actually a reference to Gama Pehelwan, who really did enjoy those dimensions, a dream of all wrestlers. All the sons of Yusuf Khan were dedicated to acquiring an awe-inspiring physique.

Not every gym rat can become an athlete. Overtraining, bad recovery of muscles, poor nutrition and weak willpower leads to the eventual burnout of many a strong man. For instance, Gerard Butler, who played the king Leonidas in the movie *300*, confessed, in one of his interviews, that he had remained sore and unwell for over a year after filming ceased. Only those who are naturally gifted and are staunchly persistent can endure and remain strong on the path. Others drop by the wayside. Similarly, one after another, the five brothers started slipping academically, which was followed by their exit from the wrestling arena as well. Shetaab, Khalil, Yaqoob and Habib were forced to cease their formal education because of inadequate attendance at school or low marks.

Everyone except Khalid Khan Pacha.

The boy remained steadfast in both métiers—academics as well as wrestling.

Khalid was also regular in the National Cadet Corps (or NCC) training at his school in Harda. The boy was fascinated with the uniform. Khalid believed that this training would be his springboard to the police force. While his father stressed on wrestling and his mother emphasized on studies, Khalid secretly nursed the desire to become a police officer.

But the hands of destiny are committed to navigate a man's life, often crushing his aspirations in a totally unexpected manner. Khalid did not have to wait too long for this; he experienced it in his teenage years.

7
The Challenger

The bucket of milk, filled to the brim and placed outside the makeshift wrestling ring, drew curious glances from all quarters.

The historical Benazir Ground, or Benazir Maidan, in Bhopal was packed to capacity with wrestling aficionados. Ram Dayal Pehelwan, who was known as the '*chattaan* of Bhopal', the unshakeable mountain, was the defender. Dayal was considered so invincible that no wrestler in his right mind ever wanted to be in the same ring as him.

In the 1960s, wrestling bouts were common in Bhopal and people gathered at Benazir Maidan to witness the spectacle of ultimate strength, tenacity and nerve in amateur wrestling competitions.

Benazir Maidan was more famous for being the venue for Mahatma Gandhi's rousing speech during his maiden visit to Bhopal in 1929, which revitalized the freedom moment in Madhya Pradesh. Nawab Hamidullah Khan, who was the ruler of the Central Provinces in pre-Independence India had invited Gandhi. It was under the aegis of the nawab's hospitality that thousands of Indians living in the Central Provinces visited Benazir Maidan to listen to Gandhi.

The legendary ground is now a dumping ground and lies in ruins and utter neglect. The Madhya Pradesh government never accorded it the respect that such a historical site and relic of the past deserved.

In 1968, thirty years after Gandhi's visit, it was used more as a wrestling arena to crown the reigning champion. Dayal had been undefeated for several years, and that day too people came to see the defeat of another wrestler at Dayal's hands. But they still came because they loved to watch the wrestling matches at Benazir Maidan, even if the fight was just a formality. They basked in Dayal's glory as he browbeat his opponents into submission.

But that year the wrestling season at Benazir Maidan was abuzz with a lot of excitement. As the season began, a rank outsider, a new fighter, who had never participated in fights before, had suddenly thrown a challenge at Ram Dayal. This had piqued everybody's interest because the upstart who had dared Dayal was a Muslim from Harda.

Madhya Pradesh has always had its share of communal flare-ups. Small incidents in the years after Independence had often escalated into full-fledged communal strife between the Hindus and Muslims.

That day, for the finals of the wrestling fest, the crowd, which generally didn't exceed 200 people, had swelled to a whopping 2000, all in a span of two hours. If you were observant, you could smell the animus among the audience.

And if the bucket of milk placed by the ring was not strange enough, five more buckets appeared. It is a Pashtun tradition to encourage brave young men, after every feat of prowess, with huge quantities of milk or almond sherbet.

This is to inspire them physically and psychologically. When a Pathan brought the first bucket of milk to the ground to cheer up the Pathan challenger, other Pathans pitched in with more buckets of milk to show solidarity with the young wrestler. The Pathan community of Bhopal were obviously very proud that it was one of their own who had decided to take on Ram Dayal. Bhopal's famous Pathans like Raees Lala and Inayat Lala carted huge tins of dried dates to the arena, towards the front row of the ring. During weddings and Eid celebrations, in their elation, Pathans would shower dry fruits or dates on the gathering. It is an Arab custom adopted by other Muslims too.

Khalid Khan Pacha, the fourth son of Yusuf Khan Pacha, was a studious and obedient boy. His father wanted him to pursue academics as well as bodybuilding. Khalid didn't disappoint his father. He was very regular with his exercise regimen. Yusuf Khan wanted all his sons to excel in wrestling and had even created a wrestling pit in his backyard. The idea was to ensure that his sons desisted from joining any other wrestler's arena, which would have been beneath his dignity. He also felt that his sons should not resort to the common, lazy excuse of 'I have no place to hone my skills.' Yusuf Khan loved all his sons but especially appreciated Khalid's tenaciousness.

Khalid Khan Pacha finished his matriculation from Harda High School and joined Saifia College in Bhopal for further studies. He was always clued-in about any wrestling news. When he learnt of the might of Ram Dayal Pehelwan, he secretly nursed a desire to vanquish him. He kept studying Ram Dayal's moves and strong points. When Khalid confided in his father that he wanted to defeat Ram Dayal, Khan senior was ecstatic. He made himself his son's coach and immediately began training him, introducing him to several special wrestling techniques in the process.

Khalid decided to take on Dayal while he was still in college. When he threw his hat in the ring, it was like the classic Hollywood moment when Rocky Balboa had sought to compete against the established champion Apollo Creed in the cult movie *Rocky*. Incidentally, Rocky was made eight years after the Khalid Khan Pacha story.

An eighteen-year-old college student challenging the reigning champion was absolutely unheard of. As the boy was a Muslim, it became a Hindu–Muslim bout. But Khalid Khan's Hindu classmates from Saifia College were also rooting for him. They liked him and felt he was the underdog.

The build-up to the contest was nail-biting. And as the tension was rising, so were communal tempers in almost every nook and corner of the city.

The organizers, however, were unfair; they created enough hurdles and complications in the league matches to ensure that Khalid would be eliminated in the initial rounds itself. Remember the wicked ways of the British referees in the film *Ip Man*, when they fabricated rules for Ip Man so he would lose the match to a conceited and arrogant British boxer? In Khalid's case, the idea was to test his skills and stamina and to really check if he was a worthy opponent for Dayal. If he was eliminated, the Hindu-majority sponsors would be more than happy to get rid of him.

But it was destined that in 1968 Khalid Khan would make his mark in life. He managed to overturn all his opponents in the league matches and stepped into the ring for the final bout against Ram Dayal Pehelwan.

Ram Dayal was known to crush his rivals within the first few seconds of grappling. But Khalid had been training for this day, this hour and this moment.

As soon as Khalid stepped into the ring, the whole makeshift stadium broke into earnest applause. Now here was a genuine contender, not some unserious upstart. Eyewitnesses recall that Ram Dayal had grudging admiration for the youth and didn't feel threatened by him. Perhaps Khalid was banking on Dayal's overconfidence, making it the first weapon in his arsenal.

After a customary handshake, both the wrestlers became immediately entangled in a battle of strength and stamina. For the first couple of minutes both kept employing the time-tested tactics and techniques of seasoned wrestlers. Experienced eyes noticed a marked difference between the approach and attitude of the two wrestlers. Dayal's moves were that of an overconfident man, as if the bout was a cakewalk, while Khalid still seemed to be playing it safe despite his dream run earlier. But Khalid was waiting for that one opportune moment to make his planned move. They both disentangled themselves and stood up on their feet to use their core strength.

It had been over two minutes and the audience was watching with bated breath. The match was not only going to decide the new champion but also which community would exult and parade the win over the other until the following year.

The world-famous 'Sparta' technique—of digging one's heels in the ground and pushing the adversary backwards with the brutal strength generated from the hips upwards, rising to the core, building up in the triceps as also the latissimus dorsi muscle and exploding through the shoulders—has been mastered by real wrestlers, taking them to glory. The secret of using this masculine strength can be understood by only a few men who have cracked the holy grail of bodybuilding.

Suddenly Khalid had a mischievous smile on his face. He moved with a particular swagger, extended his left arm behind the nape of Dayal and patted him on his trapezius muscle. Dayal, who by now was a bit irritated and was getting impatient with his rival's clichéd moves so far, was slightly distracted by the apparently childish move of this impertinent boy. Dayal fell for the stratagem and turned to see. And Khalid seemed to have waited for this moment.

Khalid crossed his leg, looping it widely across Dayal's thigh while giving him a gentle nudge. Dayal, who was yet to recover from his earlier distraction, was disoriented. This move was nowhere in the textbook of wrestlers. In a matter of nanoseconds, even before Dayal could gather his wits, Khalid lifted the mountain of Bhopal above his head. A hush fell in the stadium. It was an unbelievable spectacle. Dayal stretched his arms and legs mid-air to free himself from the iron grip of Khalid. But it was too late. Khalid had already flung him back on to the ground.

A hushed silence gripped the audience. The loudest sound that people remember hearing after that was the hard thud of Dayal landing on his back on the sand. That thud was the sweetest music to so many ears at that moment. Losing no time, Khalid jumped back on top of Dayal, giving him no time to turnover. The full-body smash on the ground marked a resounding victory. A boy had scaled the pinnacle on that winter night of 1968.

A sudden massive pandemonium erupted after that. The crowd went into a frenzy. Squeals of joy and delight filled the air.

'*O lale qurbaan! Mashallah . . . Jiyo, pacha, jiyo!* (O my diamond, I sacrifice myself for you! Wow, as Allah wished . . . Long live O king!)'

And with these loud whoops and celebratory shouting, the stadium witnessed a shower of dry fruits and dried dates on the audience. When the referee declared the verdict and announced Khalid as the winner, people saw that both the contestants were crying. In a magnanimous gesture, Dayal hugged Khalid. Surprisingly, there was no hostility between the two fighters. In the melee, some Pathans had entered the ring and forced a bucket in Khalid's hand. Khalid could not understand what was happening but that he was being forced to gulp down gallons of milk. Khalid's Hindu friends elbowed their way into the ring too and placed a huge garland around his neck. Khalid was mobbed like a hero. The event, which had generated so much animosity between the two communities all this while, was now a balm to frayed nerves.

Khalid's life changed overnight, from an anonymous college student to a popular wrestler. He began representing his college and city everywhere. He travelled to Nagpur for a lightweight wrestling championship and won the trophy.

However, this continuous participation in wrestling matches and travelling had one major casualty. Khalid, who had by now completed his graduation with a degree in economics, was not able to secure employment. Bhopal was not Mumbai, and sportsmen hardly made money in the 1960s.

Khalid was under pressure to start earning but his new-found glory as a wrestler was an impediment. In the meantime, enrolment for the Bharat Kumar Trophy in Delhi had begun. The title for Bharat Kumar and Hind Kesari is meant for heavyweight wrestlers and for college students in the lightweight category, respectively. The winner was christened Bharat Kumar.

Khalid had decided to participate in the Bharat Kumar championship and then give up wrestling to look for a more lucrative career.

In those days, Maharashtrian youths were diehard fans of wrestling and there were a couple of local *vyayamshalas* (gym schools) in most Mumbai streets, several of them established by the Shiv Sena. Some of the boys worked hard to display their strength in bodybuilding competitions while others trained to become successful wrestlers.

Though the Shiv Sena was fast gaining popularity with the Konkan Maharashtrians initially, there was nobody to sponsor the Maharashtrian boys for wrestling competitions outside Mumbai. Ironically, it was Mumbai's notorious don Ahmed Khan, alias Bashu Dada, himself a fitness enthusiast and a man with a barrel chest and rippling biceps, who became a sponsor for wrestling sports in Mumbai.

Bashu Dada believed that he was no less than the Mughal conqueror Babar, who had brought *pehelwani* (wrestling) to India. Pehelwani is a derivative of the Persian word *pehelavi*, meaning 'the front ranker', 'the proficient ones'. Babar himself had been a wrestler known for his brute physical strength. He could run a considerable distance carrying two men on either side of his shoulders! He had also been a patron of wrestling.

Even other kings and rulers in the earlier centuries enjoyed wrestling, Shivaji included. Among the saints, the Sikh guru Hargobind Singh was also known for his interest in wrestling. Among the women, Rani Lakshmibai was a reputed wrestler. There were varying styles in wrestling like *kushti* and *malla yudh* (physical combat).

In modern Maharashtra there were not many takers for physical sports. Bashu Dada loved soccer matches and freestyle wrestling. He also patronized the sports and since there were no Muslim boys who were interested in wrestling, he began sponsoring Maharashtrian youths to compete in championships. One of Bashu Dada's favourite wrestlers was a Maharashtrian college-going youth called Varun Mane. Mane turned out to be really a strong contender for the Bharat Kumar title and managed to defeat several wrestlers, seeming to be on the verge of bagging the trophy until he was face to face with Khalid Khan.

The young men continued with their throws, pins and takedowns. However, in less than two minutes, Khalid had understood that he would have to try something different with Mane, who would not give him enough time to be airlifted. Unlike north Indian contenders, Mumbai men are quick thinkers.

But Khalid figured that Mane could be confused. He decided to mislead Mane into thinking he was doing a certain move but in actuality would do something else, for which Mane would be totally unprepared. Khalid's reputation had preceded him and Mane had, of course, heard about Khalid's penchant for lifting his opponents high up in the air and flinging them to the ground. Mane had decided he would not allow Khalid to lift him up.

Khalid knew he would have to stoop this time to conquer. Suddenly, things happened in a blur. Khalid held Mane by his elbow and lunged to sit down with his knees. Mane thought this was the moment that he should be wary of, as Khalid was bracing to lift him. But Khalid was not, he was merely being deceptive. Mane tried to step back and get away from Khalid's grip. But Khalid wanted to just put his arm on Mane's thighs and hold his hamstrings tight. Mane felt gripped and immobile and was forced to capitulate. Khalid immediately lifted him on his shoulder and turned him over to the floor. Before Mane could move, Khalid dived and straddled his chest with all his weight and might. Mane was lying totally flat on the ground with a look of total disbelief in his eyes. He never expected Khalid to defeat him so easily. In wrestling this particular move is called *'kalajung dao'*—the black battle assault. Confusion, chaos and conquer.

The whole stadium rose in a standing ovation, the air reverberating with applause and whistles.

Bashu Dada was sprawled on a sofa in the front row. He was so dumbfounded at this stunning upset that he froze. He neither stood up nor joined the audience in the applause. His eyes had reddened with rage and his nostrils were flaring. He felt Khalid had been too cocky. He had no right to defeat his player in such a manner.

Bashu had taken Mane's defeat to heart. He decided to tame Khalid and subjugate him into submission.

8

The Protégé

When Khalid Khan Pacha defeated Ram Dayal Pehelwan in Bhopal and claimed the title of 'Boss of Bhopal', 777 km away, at the Ahmed Sailor High School in Nagpada, Bombay, a young boy was getting a dressing-down from his teacher. This was a regular occurrence, of course. This time, the boy had consistently failed in all the unit tests in the first semester. He was accompanied by another errant sibling, who joined him uneasily in attention as he was also the target of the teacher's ire. She finished her diatribe by summoning the boys' father to school the following day.

Police Head Constable Ibrahim Kaskar was one of the most well-respected cops in the city, working for the elite crime branch. In the 1970s, he was the most resourceful and indispensable tools in the arsenal of Mumbai Police, who commanded a lot of respect. His seniors, including the deputy commissioner of police (DCP), who were from the Indian Police Service (IPS) cadre, held him in high esteem. Kaskar and his colleagues were not treated like inferiors because they were constables, much lower down in the hierarchy. Instead, Havildar Ibrahim Kaskar solved several cases by sleuthing around and keeping his ears to the ground. He was one of the most popular in the constabulary of his time.

According to Bombay legend, he was part of the constable triumvirate, which included Pandu Havildar and Havildar 303, which was his *billa* (batch) number. Head Constable Kaskar was, however, referred to as 'Ibrahim Havildar'. He was known in police circles as an honest, devoted and extremely dedicated professional.

Among the Ibrahim Havildar stories that did the rounds, one was about how he induced fear in criminals' mind with an innocuous gesture. When Ibrahim Havildar would casually touch the brass buckle of his black leather belt, the criminals in the room would begin peeing their pants. They would often misconstrue his action because it seemed like he was about to unbuckle his belt to give them a proper thrashing until they fell unconscious. Ibrahim Havildar's seniors often tapped into this fear factor and there would be special requests for his brass-buckle trick in the interrogation room.

But Ibrahim Havildar had his own low moments. Whenever he was summoned to Ahmed Sailor High School he would break into a cold sweat. He was no longer a policeman who could terrify criminals. Instead, he felt shamed, drawn and quartered. He felt defeated and helpless, and he often asked Allah why he was being tested again and again.

Whenever his sons were up to some mischief at school, he was politely summoned by the principal. He hated to stand there before the school authorities and listen to the litany of complaints against his boys. Most of all, he wished his sons would grow up to be responsible and studious and spare him the ignominy of standing like an offender in front of the school principal. And because it was happening quite regularly, he was beginning to feel the actual pain of this whole exercise.

Fortunately, thanks to his solid police credentials, he was spared the tongue-lashing the other parents were subjected to in earfuls.

The boys would have turned out better but for an unfortunate turn of events in Ibrahim Havildar's life. Just when the children were starting out in school, he was suspended along with a batch of policemen who had investigated the death of actress Suraiya's father, Aziz Jamal Sheikh. Sheikh was found dead at his daughter's Krishna Mahal apartment in Marine Lines in 1963.

Suraiya was not just the reigning queen of the Hindi film industry but a huge sensation too. In the 1940s and 1950s, Suraiya was a top singing star and commanded a price of Rs 2 lakh per movie, at a time when other stars were being paid only in thousands. Much before the celluloid-crazy fans from south India established temples for their movie icons, Suraiya was being worshipped by fanatical fans. Her house in Marine Lines drew huge crowds and it is said that even after all these decades, her fan following and the crowds outside her house are much larger than for any of the lead actors who came in the years after her. At the zenith of her fame, on the promenade outside Marine Lines, fans would come with a *baraat* (wedding procession) and dowry, while other fans declared their eternal love and waited for a glimpse. Neither Amitabh Bachchan's home, Pratiksha, nor Rajesh Khanna's Ashirwad, nor even Shah Rukh Khan's Mannat, which receive thousands of visitors every day, witnessed such fan frenzy.

In the 1950s, Kanti Desai, the son of the then chief minister of Bombay Presidency, Morarji Desai, had once asked her to come to a private party where some political bigwigs were in attendance. Suraiya politely declined, and it is said that Kanti Desai threatened her. It's a different story that Suraiya was totally smitten with Dev Anand, to the exclusion of everybody else, and that is why her attention was elsewhere. And, then, one day, on Holi, Aziz Jamal suddenly died. Suraiya did not want her father's death to be investigated as a homicide.

It was widely alleged that Suraiya bribed the entire team of crime branch investigators to term the death a natural one. It could never be established whether the investigators obliged her for pecuniary gains, or gave in because of her cult status, as most of them were in awe of her, or whether Aziz Jamal did indeed die of natural causes.

Subsequently, the issue was raised in the state legislature. The state of Maharashtra had been newly formed and there was quite an anti-Gujarati wave being witnessed because Morarji Desai had declared that 'Maharashtra would not get Bombay in the next 5000 years.' The Samyukta Maharashtra Movement had lost over a hundred people before it won its case and Bombay finally became a part of Maharashtra. The Suraiya–Kanti Desai face-off was by then well known and the newly minted Maharashtrian politicians thought that Suraiya's father's death might reap them some windfalls. But it is well known that the moment politicians take interest in something, they look for fall guys. The entire police team probing Suraiya's father's death was suspended from service. Head Constable Ibrahim Kaskar was part of the team and was also apparently close to Suraiya's family, in a personal capacity.

Suraiya also bid adieu to a sterling movie career and signed off in 1963 with her last movie, *Rustom Sohrab*. But old-timers in the know claim that she left the movie business due to her bereavement and the subsequent controversy that forced her to retreat into a shell.

There is a proverb that says a giant tree falls to its end with a massive thud but it is the weeds and other life forms below the tree that become the collateral damage. Ibrahim Kaskar and his family were one of the biggest casualties in the wake of Suraiya's father's death. Following his three-year suspension, he was sacked from the police force in 1966. This sudden loss of his job put his large family in a precarious situation. Ibrahim Havildar had seven sons and four daughters.

Kaskar had enrolled his sons Sabir and Dawood at the English-medium Ahmed Sailor High School in Nagpada. The other children were sent to Urdu-medium municipal schools as Kaskar was suspended and could not pay the school fees regularly.

Ibrahim Havildar's best friend and cousin, Rahim Chacha, recalled how Ibrahim was nervous before every visit to the school, which was walking distance from his house in Temkar Mohalla. When the principal listed the barrage of complaints against Sabir and Dawood, including their absenteeism, consistent failure in exams and, above all, Dawood's incorrigible behaviour with his teachers and his propensity towards violence, Ibrahim could be often seen stuttering and stammering before the principal, unable to muster up a decent response.

There exist hazy apocryphal stories of how some of the victims of Ibrahim Havildar's belt treatment had threatened teachers at his sons' school to embarrass him with accounts of their misdeeds. It was said the conspirators of such complaints would stand at a distance and look at a squirming Ibrahim Havildar as he was lambasted by the teachers.

Ibrahim Havildar would return home and unleash his frustration on the boys. He beat them black and blue but they were up to their old tricks in no time. Among the two brothers, Sabir was more into roughing up his classmates, while Dawood was more into playing pranks. Their continuous mischief and physical violence had made them quite an unpopular duo in the entire school.

With an increasing number of complaints and humiliation faced at the school, Ibrahim Havildar was fast becoming disillusioned with his sons. And one fine day, when Sabir was in class eight, the inevitable happened. His worst fears came true. He was summoned to the school and told in no uncertain terms that Sabir was being rusticated as he had got into a brawl with another classmate and banged the boy's head against a bench, resulting in a serious injury that required several stitches.

Ibrahim Havildar was deeply saddened and humiliated, and brought Sabir home. Ibrahim and his wife, Amina, both now pinned their hopes on Dawood and asked him to pay attention to his studies. Dawood was in class seven and hurt by his brother's expulsion from school.

Dawood showed plenty of enthusiasm and tried to focus on his studies, knowing he was the only hope for his poor parents and starving siblings. Ibrahim's senior at the police station, Inspector Burhan Malgi used to support Ibrahim and would encourage him to let Dawood study so that eventually at least the son could join the police force as a sub-inspector. Ibrahim was grateful for Malgi's intervention and support.

Malgi prevailed on the school management to give another chance to Dawood and also promised to pay his school fees. This interest and enthusiasm shown by him facilitated Dawood's continuation of his studies and he was also inducted into the Road Safety Patrol (RSP). The initiative for including school students into the RSP, an honorary traffic-training programme for secondary-class students, was very popular. Unlike in the present times, where the RSP is totally neglected, in the 1970s it was a matter of prestige for a parent and his ward to be included in the programme.

The RSP is a programme in which schoolchildren, under the tutelage of a traffic constable, were assigned to regulate traffic in the area near their school. This would train the kids in road safety and eventually prepare them to follow law and order in the society.

Since Dawood's father had been in the traffic department for several years, Dawood was also fascinated with the police force. Subsequently, he also began visiting his father in the high-security precincts of the crime branch headquarters in Crawford Market. Right through his childhood Dawood had grown up with an abundance of uniforms around him. This had automatically resulted in two things: first, his enormous respect for and comfort with the uniform, which exuded power; and second, despite the huge respect he had for the uniform, he was not intimidated by authority. The latter helped him immensely in his criminal career.

However, his guardian angel Malgi ensured that Dawood got his RSP uniform comprising a white shirt, tie, blue shorts and a red beret cap. This immediately cheered up Dawood and his depressed father, Ibrahim Kaskar. When Dawood donned the RSP uniform, it was discussed in the family that the uniform augured well for the boy, that this was a stepping stone to other uniforms later in life and that he would not stop until he became a police officer more famous than his father. Dawood began attending the RSP training sessions regularly and also tried to improve his academic performance. The next few months were uneventful. With Sabir out of the school, Dawood was more focused. The family's expectations from him were also very high, Sabir having been written off by them. The general mood was that Dawood would turn out to be a worthy son in the Kaskar clan and change the family's fortunes through education.

But fate had other plans for Head Constable Dawood Hasan Kaskar—the khaki of the police uniform or the salute of the constables was not destined for him.

The retired assistant commissioner of police (ACP) Burhan Malgi recalled that despite his best efforts, things went beyond control after a point of time. One December morning, when Dawood was manning the Nagpada Junction, opposite Sarvi restaurant, he suddenly got distracted at the sight of a few boys assembling outside the garden at the end of the Clare Road intersection that merges at Nagpada Junction.

Dawood was standing in the middle of the intersection and trying to whistle and navigate the huge inflow of traffic, but he kept looking at the boys who had now formed a group and had some sticks and rods in their hands. Dawood could not understand the strange behaviour of the boys. Soon they disappeared from his sight.

Ahmed Sailor High School had a full-fledged basketball team that practised regularly. Sabir was good at basketball and used to participate regularly when he was in school. Even after his suspension, he would go and just watch the matches, sitting on the school wall. His detractors never liked his presence around the school.

One particular day, there happened to be one player short on the court. Sabir's friend asked him to substitute for an injured player. Sabir gladly joined the team. In a span of a few minutes, he had managed to score a couple of baskets. The opposing team did not like this and shoved him a couple of times. Initially, Sabir shrugged it off, but when he saw a pattern, he kicked one of the boys in the groin. This immediately escalated matters.

A secret message was circulated by the opposing team and a few boys were summoned as reinforcements to rein in Sabir. It was this group of boys that Dawood had earlier seen from his spot at Nagpada Junction. In less than half an hour, Dawood had received word that a group of boys had cornered Sabir and assaulted him. Dawood abandoned his post and rushed to his brother's aid. The school was barely 500 metres away and Dawood made it to the ground in no time.

Dawood reached the playground and was taken aback to see his worst fears coming true. One of the boys had hit Sabir on his head with a stick from behind. This sudden assault had startled Sabir and he had fallen down. As he plummeted to the ground, other boys who had been hiding appeared and began showering him with kicks and punches. Sabir screamed helplessly, desperately trying to protect himself.

Dawood could not remain a spectator any longer. He threw his whistle, flung his cap away and ran towards the boys, hurling himself at the group of boys beating his brother up. It was an uneven fight, in which Sabir and Dawood were outnumbered and outmanoeuvred by their rivals. The struggle continued for a few minutes and both the brothers sustained lot of injuries and cuts on their faces and bodies.

Dawood too had managed to inflict some grievous injuries on one of the boys before they could be separated. Sabir had suffered some injuries too, his lips were torn and his face was bleeding.

The issue had become grave and a group of parents descended on to the school the following day. They wanted a police case filed against the brothers and demanded that they should be thrown in a children's home. This time, despite Malgi's intervention, the irate parents were not willing to listen.

In the meanwhile, Dawood, who was too scared to face his teachers, decided to bunk school for a couple of days—which turned into weeks and, finally, months. Eventually, Dawood joined the ranks of school dropouts and began spending the day loafing around the streets. His degeneration towards a criminal life had begun at an accelerated pace.

While Ibrahim Kaskar was struggling to make both ends meet and help his starving, impoverished family, he was unable to focus on his wayward sons, who were too busy with their own delinquent ways.

Ibrahim's promising young lads thus bid adieu to their academic career and veered towards a life of joblessness and crime. He used to keep receiving complaints against them, and he wanted to ensure their reformation, but he just could not do enough to straighten them out.

Once again, he sought help from Malgi, who summoned Dawood and attempted to admonish him, saying, 'One fight should not be the reason for abandoning your studies.'

'We did not start the fight. We were attacked by a whole bunch of boys who had come prepared to beat Sabir up. We were beaten up. We only tried to defend ourselves,' Dawood told Malgi in an uncharacteristic outburst.

'You need to just apologize to the parents and the boys. And all this will be over. You will be back to school,' Malgi tried to convince him.

'*We* are the victims. *We* deserve an apology. Why should *we* apologize?' Dawood retorted.

And now that the floodgates were open, Dawood continued, 'I wish we could have fought like film heroes, where the hero faces several villains at once and still emerges victorious. I wanted to punch that Umar Saand [bull] and Sufiyan Mental. It is only because I am helpless without the requisite fighting skills that I got beaten up. Can you train me in physical combat which might come handy in such situations?' Dawood asked innocently.

Years later, Malgi is still not able to forget Dawood's innocence and rage.

Malgi tried to reason with Dawood that there was no reason for him to learn hand combat, and that it was not a career option for him. 'Such physical violence will lead you to jail,' he had warned the boy.

Dawood had respect for Malgi, of course. But he knew that he did not like being beaten up or pushed into a corner. He realized he wanted the upper hand in all situations—always. Dawood had already made up his mind to be a fighter. All he needed was a coach to fulfil his dream.

9

Khalid: Bashu's Acolyte

A gleaming red Mercedes Pagoda was sliding down the road towards the J.J. Junction. In the 1970s, it was a rare sight. Except for film actors, business tycoons and affluent car-crazy Parsis, nobody else thought of importing a Mercedes-Benz to India, what with the added headache of the staggering customs tariff. The car was a true status symbol. And that was exactly what made it a rare sight in this part of town.

From the moment the Pagoda made its appearance on the road, it was a showstopper. Everyone on the street—right from the pedestrians to the shopkeepers, to bystanders and other car drivers—stopped to admire the beautiful two-seater Mercedes coupé. The residents and passers-by knew that Ahmed Khan, better known as Bashu Dada, was on the prowl. Much before other smugglers and businessmen from Dongri had switched to the luxury Mercedes cars, Bashu Dada had cruised around in one and made it a point to flaunt it among the lesser mortals of the area.

Whenever Bashu Dada stepped outside, everybody in the neighbourhood knew it was wise to stay out of his way. Bashu

Dada was well known for his foul temper and arrogance. The man was stockily built, broadly muscular, and always wore half-sleeved shirts, or a safari suit, so that his biceps were always visible. He had long hair à la Sunil Dutt in those days, which covered his nape and neck, with long, thick sideburns running down to his lower cheeks. He rarely smiled.

Before Dawood became a 'Bhai' and gave a whole new lexicological twist to the word, the local hoodlum and strongman was addressed as 'Dada'. While in Marathi it meant 'elder brother', in several Maharashtrian families the word was used to refer to one's father. In northern India, 'dada' meant 'grandfather', while in Bengali, it was used to mean 'elder brother'. In north Indian households, one would often say, '*Hum tere baap ke bhi baap hain* (I am a father to your father)' to children and youngsters, reflecting a chauvinistic, alpha male outlook.

So Bashu Dada was, in a manner of speaking, the father of all the humble subjects in his fiefdom. He would never bend down to tie his shoelaces; his acolytes would do the needful. If a police officer had to serve summons to him, he would have to park his vehicle at the entrance of Hujra Mohalla, walk the distance to Bashu's *akhara* (wrestling pit)—smack in the middle of the city—respectfully remove his cap and politely convey the court's order to him. It was left to Bashu's whim about whether he would accept the summons, respond to the court directive or just dismiss it disdainfully with a wave of his hand.

Bashu used to occasionally ride in his Mercedes to survey the city, catch up with his people and also to make an ugly display of his power and pelf. Khalid was sitting next to Bashu, looking at the hustle and bustle of the city with delight. He was extremely happy to have been seated in such an expensive car alongside one of the most powerful men of Bombay. Like his grandfather, who was a loyal man Friday to the reigning Nawab of Bhopal, Khalid was indispensable to Bashu.

Khalid had witnessed Bashu's clout in the area, the way policemen saluted him and how even the mighty trembled in his presence. All in all, he was pleased with his decision to accept Bashu's job offer soon after the Delhi fight. After Khalid defeated Bashu's favourite wrestler, Mane, Bashu approached him. Khalid, who had grown up watching his grandfather at the service of a rich nawab, thought he could do the same. He thought Bashu was a seth, and Bombay the ticket for a better life. Despite having completed his education, Khalid was not sure about his vocation. Secure government jobs were aplenty for a graduate but Khalid did not want to waste his life as a pen-pusher. He knew that pehelwani would not give him a stable income, but he had been told that his physique and education might help him secure a police inspector's post. Khalid did his homework and learnt that the Madhya Pradesh government had planned a drive for police recruitment in a couple of months' time. He made up his mind to appear for the tests and try his luck with the Bhopal Police. At that point of time, he was yet to come to Bombay or experience it. Bhopal was his home and hearth, and whatever plans he had in life revolved around the city. When Bashu Dada made the job offer, Khalid thought it was his chance to see Bombay, all-expenses paid, and return to Bhopal for the police job. There were still a few months left before the recruitment.

Once in Bombay, Khalid realized that Bashu was the uncrowned king of Dongri. But what surprised Khalid was the attitude of the police. He always thought the uniform of the police made them distinct individuals, vesting them with power and authority. But in Bombay he was surprised to see the police being subservient to Bashu. If a police officer wanted to meet Bashu, who happened to be watching a soccer match on TV, the officer would have to wait patiently until the end of the match. Nothing could interrupt the match, not even a uniformed on-duty police officer. This servile and slavish attitude of the cops disappointed him, and Khalid's respect for khaki took a beating.

On the other hand, Khalid was drawn to Bashu's power. Bashu Dada regaled him with stories of his bravery and of how he had managed to hold his own against all his foes. Khalid was impressed. He was moving away from his goal of becoming a police officer.

On that particular day in August 1971, when Bashu had begun his tour of the area with Khalid in tow, he started telling him about his elder brother, Mohammad Khan. 'After losing my parents early in life, all I had as family was my brother. But a dada from the neighbouring mohalla, Hassu Maharaj, got him drunk and stabbed him to death when he was alone at night.'

It had been over a year since his brother had been killed but Khalid realized that Bashu Dada's grief was still very raw. Every time he mentioned his brother his eyes went moist.

Hassu Maharaj was a mean, insolent, legitimate street ruffian. He had several murder cases, extortion and cases of attempted murders (in legal parlance known as 'half murder' in those days) registered against him. Hassu was jealous of Bashu because of his wealth, his connections with the police and his flashy car, his badam-sherbet machine and his akhara. Hassu also hired more toughies in his gang to convey his power. Gangs are run by muscles and machines, and more men means more power and a bigger fear-factor.

Bashu was the short form of 'Badshah', which means 'emperor'. Not to be outdone, Hassu added the tag of 'Maharaj', to signify his status as king. They had several altercations about their men and violations of turf. Finally, Hassu decided to settle scores personally and cunningly trapped and killed Bashu's brother. Bashu was distraught. For days he did not leave his house and spent most of his time mourning his brother.

'Why didn't you take revenge?' Khalid often asked Bashu Dada.

'Soon after the murder, the police became proactive. They realized that the murder could escalate into a gang war in the city, so they immediately arrested Hassu and put him behind bars.'

At the Arthur Road Jail, Bashu used all his influence to deny material comforts to Hassu, including good food, blankets and hot water. In fact, some of Bashu's men serving time in jail also picked up deliberate fights with Hassu and roughed him up. These reports of the continuous harassment and humiliation of his brother's killer were music to Bashu's ears. However, all this only made Hassu more vindictive towards Bashu, and he vowed that he would wait for his turn to get back at Bashu.

'So he killed my brother one day. And I am killing him every day . . . and will keep killing him till he actually dies . . .' Bashu's words trailed off.

Thunkkkkk!

A big, loaded handcart had dashed against his car and badly dented the shining bonnet of his Mercedes. He was forced to bring the car to a screeching halt. Bashu was furious. He immediately opened the door and rushed out to see the extent of the damage. Khalid also opened his side of the car door and stepped out.

The sight that welcomed the two beefcakes was daunting in every sense. Some eight men had surrounded the car. All of them had sharp knives and *gupti*s (choppers) in their hands.

They seemed to be dangerous and ready to kill. Hassu Maharaj stood at the helm, sporting a devilish grin.

Unbeknown to Bashu, Hassu had managed to secure bail and had gathered all his mean minions to ambush Bashu when he passed by his area.

'*Chal Bashu tujhe tere bhai ke paas pahuncha deta hoon* (Come, Bashu, I shall dispatch you to keep company with your dead brother),' Hassu said and slowly took a step towards Bashu. It was clear that he was ready to assault and kill Bashu. Hassu was slow because he was also wary and alert; he didn't know whether Bashu had a gun tucked under his belt. But Bashu had nothing.

Bashu, who maintained his aplomb, was extremely nervous from within. Was this the end? However, he leaned towards Khalid and whispered, '*Aaj mera saath de do, bhai* (Brother, stand by me today).'

Khalid had never before been into knife fights. Apart from wrestling, Khalid had only been involved in hockey-stick fights in college, which were more about power play and dominance and not intended to kill. But the men facing him were armed with lethal weapons and had dangerous designs, a situation which was totally alien for Khalid despite all his bravura. But Bashu's plea jolted him to the core and he felt pity for the loneliness of a bereaved brother who was also his boss and his ticket to a good life in the city. Khalid's pity turned into anger towards his crony's enemy, which was further fuelled into rage by the unfairness of it all. Suddenly Khalid felt a sudden flow of high-octane strength streaming into his veins and his muscles felt ready to explode with raw force.

He called out to Bashu, '*Bhai, aap Hassu ko dekho, main baaki haramzado ko jahannum bhejta hoon* (Brother, you take care of Hassu; I will send the others to hell),' and with that he pounced on the closest adversary. Khalid held the wrist of the man who had the knife but did not twist it, as it would have meant facing resistance and giving the others a chance to attack him while he would be busy pinning the man down. Rather, he pulled the man with full force and rammed his face against the roof of the car. This happened in a blur. Nobody understood what had happened until they heard the loud sound. The man's skull had hit the red Mercedes and made it redder with the blood that was gushing from his eyebrows and seeping into his eyes.

The other man rushed towards Khalid, heaving the chopper in the air so that he could it bring down on Khalid's chest and rip his heart out. But Khalid held the armed hand and, using a wrestler's stance of lowering himself to the chest of his opponent and lifting him over his shoulder, knocked the man on the ground, face down, before he could even figure out what was happening, resulting in a broken nose and several knocked-out teeth.

The two quick casualties in the enemy camp emboldened Bashu. He felt encouraged enough to take on Hassu with more ferociousness. Bashu advanced towards Hassu; using his head as a weapon, he hit hard on Hassu's chin. Taken aback by this attack, Hassu collapsed on the ground, sprawled on his back. Bashu was blind with fury as he channelled his love for football and began kicking Hassu mercilessly all over his body with his pointed shoes. The air reverberated with Hassu's screams.

In the meanwhile, like the modern-day Hulk, Khalid had effortlessly lifted a couple of more men on his shoulder and, using his wrestler's trick, thrown them on the handcart and flung some on the motorcycles parked on the side of the road. Their ribs must have broken from the force and impact of the fall. Hassu's men were being thrown around like loose gunny sacks by a rampaging bull-like man who seemed to have gone berserk. In a matter of minutes, the whole fight had been overturned to Bashu's advantage. The last two men from Hassu's team saw a possessed Khalid with his modus operandi of breaking heads, snapping noses, cracking ribs and spreading blood all over the tar road. They also saw their ringleader, Hassu, being kicked relentlessly and rolling over with pain and agony. They decided not to mess with Khalid that day and instead run for their lives. They pushed away the crowd of spectators and ran off.

Bashu kept kicking Hassu and it seemed like he would kill his rival that day. Khalid warned Bashu, 'There are too many witnesses and it is not a good idea to kill Hassu in full public view.'

'I want to kill him today in front of the whole world to teach him a lesson,' Bashu thundered.

Eventually, Khalid prevailed. There was an air of awe and appreciation at Khalid's heroics. Khalid was happy with himself and walked with a certain swagger. Winning a duel in the ring with one man, bound by certain rules, is different from vanquishing a group of violent men on the street. Wrestling is a sport, beating street goons single-handedly is heroism.

The spectators had begun dispersing and the crowd was thinning gradually. Bashu turned and hugged Khalid and was full of gratitude and praise for his new acolyte. He felt vindicated at his decision of hiring Khalid. Everyone was gone, Hassu had also managed to get up and slink away from the scene. Dusk was setting in. The traffic on the road was increasing. Some cops had arrived on the scene. They saw Bashu and stopped in their tracks.

Khalid was ready to leave and about to get into the car. His mind was racing furiously. Would this ruin his prospects of joining the police force? Should he choose Bombay over his home town, Bhopal? This fight might have given him a high, but would it change his destiny? Khalid could not be more mistaken or wrong. The destiny changer was not the fight itself, it was an absolutely unlikely and unrelated phenomenon standing a few metres away from the spot.

At the mouth of Temkar Mohalla stood a transfixed teenager in an ordinary shirt and shorts, but with an extraordinary glint in his eyes.

Dawood Ibrahim had found his hero, his role model, his paragon of power. He was in awe of Khalid's agile movements, lightning-quick reflexes and brute strength. And understandably so. What Khalid had displayed was incredible. He had neutralized and vanquished armed and dangerous men. Dawood thought this was only possible in the movies. But this man was real. Dawood wanted to approach him and persuade him to take him under his tutelage. But he was so astonished and inspired by Khalid that his legs felt glued to the spot.

Khalid, who had opened the car door and was getting in, noticed the boy. There was something about him that was compelling. Khalid noticed the boy looking at him with a rapt and unblinking gaze. He decided to break the ice and gave him a wide smile.

Dawood was now totally floored, his hero had acknowledged him with a generous smile.

Who knew this brief meeting was going to be the foundation of a long-lasting and unbreakable bond between them.

10

Dangerous Man, Dangerous Mind

The movement of the torchlight was clear and vivid. In the pitch darkness, the systematic and well-co-ordinated movement of light was unmissable. The torch moved in a slow, fluid movement, forming the capital letter *B* with the light; then, after a brief break, it made the Hindi letter *ba* and then the Urdu letter *bey*.

This was not part of some choreographed sound and light show taking place at a heritage monument. It was actually a subtle signal being transmitted to an Arab dhow in the high seas, which was waiting to move forward and get closer. The dhow operator, who was watching this light signal of the illuminated B, ba and bey, through his binoculars, was satisfied with the cipher.

This was an indication that the men in the boat were from Bashu Dada's gang. The B was a signal meant to show their group affiliation. When the dhow came closer, the seven men from the vessel intoned: '*Arabi maal, Dubai ki dhamaal* (Goods from Arabia, fun from Dubai).' In response, Bashu's men chorused back: '*Bashu Bambai ka badshah* (Bashu is the emperor of Bombay).' The preprogrammed code was a safety measure to rule out the presence of customs cops or rival gangs who could have weaselled out the consignment from right under their nose.

Once the contact and codes were established and verified, the two groups started transferring the consignment from the dhow to the smaller fishing boats—huge rectangular slabs of silver weighing 35 kg each, called the 'silver brick', or *chaandi ki eenth*. Each boat could handle a maximum of seventy bricks, but since the journey was short from the middle of the sea to the shore, the fear of capsizing was less. Once ashore, the silver bricks were quickly transported to a jeep or a tempo. The dhow normally carried 500 bricks, and it took all night for the bricks to be loaded on to the fishing boat and then on to the vehicle on the shore.

Bashu and Khalid were on the shore, supervising the whole operation. They oversaw the loading of the silver on to the jeeps by the burly men. Their presence on shore was crucial for them in several ways: if at all they were in danger of a surprise raid by customs or police officers, they would be able to easily escape from the shore after sensing trouble from afar.

If Khalid was awestruck by the whole episode, he didn't show it. It was the first time for him. The first time he had discovered that Bashu smuggled silver and not gold. By now he had, of course, realized that Bashu was not a legitimate businessman. In the 1960s and 1970s, smuggling was considered a shortcut to riches. And Bashu was very rich. But Khalid never asked, and it took a while for Bashu to take him into confidence. He was also to learn that Bashu was not exactly a smuggler but only a landing agent.

Khalid was an economics graduate and he understood business economics and logistics better than the illiterate

Bashu. The calculations that Bashu shared with Khalid were mind-boggling. Silver, as compared to gold, was a cheaper metal but each brick earned a margin of Rs 10,000–15,000, depending on market trends. Every silver consignment easily translated into a massive profit of over 50 lakh. After greasing the palms of corrupt customs officials and other irritants, they would still make a clean profit of Rs 25 lakh, which was a phenomenal figure in the early 1970s. And by a conservative estimate, even if they made four landings a year, they would stand to pocket a cool Rs 1 crore. And to think that he wanted to work as a policeman on a salary of Rs 500 per month. Khalid laughed when he thought about where his life could have gone.

Bashu and Khalid got into his Mercedes after the goods were loaded into waiting tempos and jeeps. It was a long journey of over 172 km from Vapi in Gujarat to Bombay. En route, Bashu explained the intricacies of the trade and the advantages of dealing in silver and not gold: 'I want to seize the lion's share in the bullion market,' he boasted.

Bashu told Khalid about his connections in Dubai and also about other landing spots near Raigad and on the Gujarat coasts. Khalid listened attentively. He instinctively felt drawn towards this business. Smuggling did not seem like a sin. There was no bloodshed involved; it did not feel like a crime. Khalid came from a world far removed from criminality and wrongdoing. He knew that once he stepped into this territory, it would be a world very different from the world he was accustomed to, of nobility and nawabs. It would be goodbye to the genteel way of life that he grew up with.

But who could resist the lure of money. It was not a small sum but a massive jackpot available for the picking. No other business or enterprise could fetch so much money in one go.

Khalid decided to master the business. He realized that Bashu had his own shortcomings and could handle the business only on a limited scale despite his background and muscle power.

If Khalid were to make improvements to the business, he would first have to zero in on the most obvious lacunae. He felt it was important to be a smuggler—not a landing agent. It is the smuggler who controls both the consigner and the consignee and therefore reaps the maximum windfall in the deal. He also felt that Bashu should make inroads into gold smuggling. Khalid possessed a sharp business acumen and began exploring permutations and combinations to take their dealings further. An illiterate criminal is harmful but an educated criminal is fatally dangerous, almost lethal. Khalid's inclination and aspiration to become a smuggler would eventually put a dent in the already doddering Indian economy.

It was the Indo-China war in 1962 that drove home the extent of the foreign-exchange drain. The opening up of the economy and allowing a liberal trade regime to flourish was simply not in the government's scheme of things. The then finance minister, Morarji Desai, who was with the Congress at the time, blamed it on gold. Over the next seven years he introduced a series of steps that he thought would help rein in the problem. The Gold Control Act was introduced. From banning the production of gold jewellery above 14 carats to introducing gold bond schemes with taxes exempt for unaccounted wealth, he tried everything. But nothing worked. Finally, the Gold Control Act of 1968 came into force, which forbade citizens from owning gold in the form of bars and coins. It was a draconian law that impinged on the right of an individual to secure his own future by hoarding gold. It became mandatory for those in possession of gold bars to melt it to make gold jewellery and even declare the same to the government. Goldsmiths too faced a massive crackdown from the government. They could not own more than 100 gm of gold and even licensed gold dealers could not own more than 2 kg of gold. Gold trading was banned. Under those circumstances, the legal market for gold simply vanished overnight as the underground market flourished.

Financial experts and economists believe that we lost a decade of economic progress because, given our government's obsession with gold, we lost out on other economic opportunities and, worse, compounded our economic woes with the rampant smuggling of gold and silver from those Gulf nations that had a liberal gold policy.

Imagine, had this gold 'smuggling' been legalized between the years 1970 and 1992, gold would have accounted for 70 per cent of the imports into India. Instead, the Indian government was battling the fallout of gold smuggling, like hawala rackets and other money-laundering schemes that were being used to pay for the illegally imported gold into the country.

After Bashu dozed off in the car, Khalid's mind was spinning furiously. He was thinking hard to strategize and come up with a fantastic plan that would impress Bashu and multiply their profits. Finally, when they reached their house in Telli Galli, Khalid had made his decision. But there was a problem with his plan. Khalid was ambitious and gutsy but he lacked market-related knowledge and experience. He wanted to crack this conundrum and realized that he needed to think more on the subject to be able to arrive at a solution.

By the time they got to their respective rooms and hit their beds, the sun was up. Khalid was unable to manage a restful sleep. He was tossing and turning in bed, struggling to sleep, and even though he was tired, he could not disconnect totally from the web of his thoughts. Sleep experts firmly believe that one should not take stressful thoughts to bed as they may hamper sleep. However, Roman scholars and Greek philosophers have their own interpretation of the same. Aristotle, who is revered in Indian literature as Arastu, had opined that men are capable of attaining clear wisdom only during sleep because it is only then that their minds are totally unshackled and free. One hears of people who often wake up in the morning bursting with a creative idea that becomes the roadmap of their life.

Khalid, too, was jolted awake because of a commotion outside. He wondered why, considering it was a Sunday and people like to sleep in longer on holidays. But the tumult and noise in the street forced him out of his bed. As he got up, he was hit with inspiration—an idea that became the solution to his riddle as well as the decision for his next step. This would give final shape to his plans for smuggling.

Khalid immediately dressed in a tight T-shirt and trousers, combed his long, curly hair and came out on the street. He was faced with a bizarre spectacle.

Two huge ostriches were locked in an adversarial stance, in full face-off mode, and were being coaxed to fight against each other. They were surrounded by a crowd of shouting and cheering men. There were also bets being placed on this fight. This looked like a scene straight out of Waziristan, where cockfights ruled the day. It was a picture of high energy, chaos and enthusiasm. It took a while for Khalid to figure out that once every three months, the Mumbai Pathans would go berserk with this ostrich showdown, a hand-me-down from their forefathers. While south Bombay's rich jumped at the prospect of horse racing, the city's other powerful men, mostly from the mafia, flexed their muscles through ostrich fights.

Khalid had never witnessed such a spectacle in his life. In fact, he had not even heard of this kind of fight between two birds. He had also not known about a turkey fight, which was very common those days. Ostrich fighting, on the other hand, is a different ball game altogether. The ostrich is a heavy bird and has a minimum weight of 100 kg. Its kick can kill an animal and even a man.

Khalid had heard of ostrich-racing competitions in Dubai, in which people rode on ostriches like jockeys on horses, after fixing the saddles, stirrups and reins. The races were considered to be quite interesting, sometimes even thrilling, with exciting photo finishes, just like in horse races. According to ornithologists, wild ostriches were prone to getting involved in territorial fights in order to gain supremacy and secure the right to including female ostriches in their group to ensure multiple mating facilities. The ostriches were capable of killing each other with merely a strong thrust of their heads.

Khalid saw that the ostrich's necks were shaved so that each hit or bruise could be considered a score point in the competition. The fight continued for barely fifteen minutes before a referee intervened and the birds were separated. One of them was declared the winner. Before he could fathom what was about to happen, four men walked with a sack towards the apparently defeated bird, tied up its feet and neck, bundled it up and took it away.

Bashu, who had seen a flummoxed Khalid watching the fight confusedly, walked up to him and animatedly told him: 'The fight is called *shuturmurg* kushti [ostrich wrestling]. It is much more interesting than human wrestling. And now we are going to have biryani made with ostrich meat, from the losing bird, and it will be far more delicious and bursting with protein than any other meat you may have had so far.'

While Khalid half-heartedly heard Bashu out, he was impatient to tell him about the grandiose plans he had been contemplating through the night since their return from Vapi. As he was about to speak up, Bashu turned towards him and introduced Khalid to a middle-aged man.

'*Yeh Ibrahim Bhai hain, yeh police mein head constable the* (This is Ibrahim Bhai, he used to be a head constable in the police) . . . He wanted to meet you,' said Bashu.

Khalid was totally mystified by this introduction. It seemed to be a friendly meeting and Ibrahim Bhai seemed to be a courteous and affable man, but why on earth would he want to meet Khalid? Khalid turned towards him and greeted him, '*Salaam alaikum,*' also shaking hands with him.

'*Walaikum salaam, aap se milkar bahut khushi hui* (It is very nice to meet you),' Ibrahim Bhai replied. And he did seem genuinely happy to be meeting Khalid.

Then Ibrahim said something that further astonished Khalid: 'My son Dawood was praising you highly after your heroic fight with the goondas last week. He wanted to meet you and shake hands with you and has been pestering his mother, asking her to intercede on his behalf. He desperately wanted to meet you.' Ibrahim Bhai's humility and sincerity was touching.

Khalid had not met such a modest and down-to-earth man—someone who enjoyed an excellent reputation in the force, was widely respected in the society and yet was so gentle and warm with a total stranger.

Khalid looked at the young boy with long unkempt hair, but one could not miss the glint in his eyes. The boy's face was shining, it was as if he were meeting his idol. There was fascination writ large on his face.

Dawood was immediately impressed with Khalid's persona: long hair, tight T-shirt with short sleeves accentuating his biceps and pectoral muscles; also noticeable were his strong, muscular thighs and well-shaped calf muscles. The boy suddenly realized that he was expected to say something; he immediately blurted out, 'Khalid Bhai, *salaam alaikum*.'

Khalid greeted him back and gave him a wide grin.

This was the first introduction between Khalid and Dawood—it was the first time the mentor and the protégé ever shook hands.

As Khalid turned to look for Bashu again, to continue his conversation about his new plans, Dawood held out his hand and said, '*Khalid Bhai, mujhe aap ki tarah banna hai, aap ke jaisa fight karna hai* (I want to be like you, I want to fight like you).'

Khalid turned towards him perfunctorily, saying, '*Haan haan, kyon nahin, bilkul sikha denge* (Absolutely, I will teach you).'

But then, suddenly, Khalid left the spot, even as Dawood continued gaping at him. Khalid located Bashu and took him aside. Bashu was holding a 555 cigarette between his fingers and was about to light it but Khalid's confident and elaborate strategy took his breath away. As Khalid kept talking, Bashu looked at him totally stunned. Bashu had presumed that Khalid was all brawn and no brain. But Khalid's ambitious plans and his blueprint for smuggling showed him another side to the man. While he was impressed with Khalid's intelligence, there was another emotion that was overriding the awe. Bashu realized that Khalid was not as simple as he seemed. He was quite a complex man with unbridled ambitions. A dangerous man with a very dangerous mind.

11

The Galadari Touch

The throne-like chairs with their ornate work and imposing presence did not deflect from the presence of those occupying it. The Galadari brothers of Dubai seemed aristocratic. They looked authoritative, and their home exuded regalia. They were listening raptly to an Indian seated on a sofa.

Their large drawing room, Khalid Pehelwan noted, was so large that it could fit all of Teli Mohalla inside it. The Galadaris lived in a palatial house. When a liveried steward floated in with the food trolley, Khalid noticed the expensive silverware and the hard silver sheet that adorned the tabletop.

As Khalid's glance fell on the fittings and fixtures made of pure silver, he compared them with Bombay's rich who thought they were a cut above the rest even if they had only had brass doorknobs like common folk.

Khalid had sat before them for over an hour, discussing the prospect of becoming the sole, exclusive gold-smuggling agents for the Galadaris. He was feeling overdressed and irritated at his beige-coloured safari suit with two big square pockets on the chest. He could not have possibly worn his half-sleeved shirts or a T-shirt, meant to display his muscular biceps. He wanted to be taken seriously—as a businessman with a proposition—and not as a badass from the big bad streets of Bombay.

It was October 1972 when a major port called Rashid, built by a British company, was inaugurated in Dubai. Khalid decided that this was his most opportune moment to make a trip to Dubai and had convinced Bashu about his plans.

Khalid's logic and rationale persuaded Bashu to take the leap. A not-so-literate Bashu had always focused on silver bricks and would have been content with a few lakh rupees in his pocket. In the 1970s, it was, of course, quite an enormous sum. But Khalid was ambitious and thought a bigger canvas to operate on would make them billionaires in a jiffy. He was an economics graduate and he spoke to Bashu about the return on investment (ROI) factor. The ROI, which decides the lucrative aspect of any enterprise, was his decisive argument that made Bashu buckle.

The plan was simple. Khalid told Bashu that if they dealt in gold smuggling, which was less voluminous, the profits would be huge, while silver bricks brought in lesser profits unless you smuggled it in bulk. The overheads were the same for both gold and silver, with the same huge sums allocated for bribing the policemen and customs officers. He pointed out that they earned only a 25 per cent profit margin in silver, but with gold smuggling they could net in 100 per cent. India's Gold Control Act had made gold a scarce commodity. From jewellers to consumers to hoarders, everybody wanted gold that they wouldn't need to declare to the government. While the demand for gold was soaring, the supply channel was weak and inconsistent.

'If we facilitate a steady supply of gold in the market, we will have the prime mover advantage and will be the masters of the game,' he announced to a stunned Bashu.

Khalid's pitch was so powerfully perfect that Bashu found no need to question or dissuade him. What they needed was a partner on the other end who would regularly send gold to them. Khalid then offered to make a trip to Dubai, from where most of the gold was smuggled to India at the time.

After some initial hesitation, Bashu gave in and allowed Khalid to make a trip to Dubai. Bashu had made some calls through a chain of middlemen and organized a meeting with the Galadaris, who were among the legions of Iranians who had migrated to Dubai over a century ago.

Abdul Wahab, Abdul Latif and Abdul Rahim Galadari were among the elite Arab families of Iranian origin in Dubai. Hailing from the predominantly Sunni populace in the southern region of Galadar village in Shiite Iran, the brothers had made quite a fortune in a short time. Iran and Dubai enjoyed amiable relations, and migration was easier and convenient on both sides of the borders.

Leaving behind their homeland Iran, the Galadaris had migrated to Dubai in the 1960s. During their teenage years, the brothers worked odd jobs to eke out a living. In fact, Abdul Wahab started working at the British Bank of the Middle East in 1964 as a clerk. Despite the humble beginning, it was still a job in a prestigious multinational bank. The first principle he learnt was: 'Contacts Get You Contracts'. He also developed other axioms by combining English and Arabic, such as, 'Risk Mein Rizq Hai, meaning 'when you take risks, you enhance your sustenance'.

Within a couple of years, Abdul Wahab had developed a wide network of contacts, retaining his hunger for more.

Wahab redefined the term 're-export'. The idea was to make a list of all the products that were coming to Dubai at a cheaper price from places such as the US, Japan and Europe, and which could still be forwarded onwards to third-world countries at a good margin. These products had a huge demand in India, Pakistan, Bangladesh and other countries of the subcontinent where governments followed the policy of protectionism to help local businesses.

Abdul Wahab re-exported watches, transistors, electronic goods, fabrics and other fancy items to India, Pakistan and Bangladesh through the smuggling corridor. Toshiba and Rado, music stereo systems, vinyl discs, clothes, yards of glistening polyester fabric, crystalware and porcelain were all the rage with Indians in the 1970s. But there was one item that excited Abdul Wahab the most and that was gold. The yellow metal was his favourite. But little did he know that it would lead to his eventual doom.

In fact, Wahab was a pioneer of gold and silver smuggling from Dubai to Pakistan, and later to India, way back in 1964, even before the UAE came into existence. Galadari's gold was legendary among jewellers, and Wahab often personally sailed with the dhow that carried the smuggled gold to Karachi and Bombay. Wahab was extremely smart and realized early on that the international markets wanted silver, which was used in many industries, including films. So he brought the metal to the gold-obsessed countries of India and Pakistan, and took away silver from these countries to sell to the Western powers for a huge profit. In India, he and his brothers were wanted men, as the DRI, India's premier anti-smuggling enforcement agency had issued a lookout notice for them.

Actually, the Galadari brothers were lucky that they lived in a part of the world that was open to trading relations with other countries. And they were fortunate that a series of political alignments happened at the right time. Dubai was still in its infancy, with the Trucial States having won their freedom from British administration in 1971. The UAE, a union of states, was born in 1971 after six states, including Dubai, Abu Dhabi, Sharjah, Ajman, Umm Al Quwain and Fujairah, had formed a union. After Iran annexed the islands of Tunbs and BuMusa, Ras al-Khaimah too became insecure and joined the group of states, making them a group of seven, in February 1972.

Dubai had discovered oil just six years prior to these developments, in 1966. In fact, till 1973, it did not even have its own currency. The people were using the Qatari rial for monetary transactions, with the Dubai dirham being introduced only in 1973. At the time, the population of Dubai was not even 200,000 people, excluding the expatriates. Any business in Dubai was an inevitable success because the place was a tax haven. In 1970s Dubai, there were two groups of *taajirs*, or traders. There were the business tycoons who had come from Iran. And then there were the local Arab traders with shops in the souk, called the Watnis, the locals. Both the Arab and Pakistani businessmen believed smuggling was permissible. In fact, the word 'smuggling' is absent in the Arabic lexicon.

The Galadaris were very rich, and when Khalid approached them, they were one of the handful of families with access to the ruler Sheikh Rashid bin Saeed Al Maktoum. The Maktoums, in those days, were accessible to their subjects and had not yet developed the arrogance of the subsequent generations. The local Arabs, who were referred to as Watnis, derivative of the word *watan*, which, in the Indian context, could be interpreted as 'sons of the soil', hated the guts of the Galadaris, who they thought were outsiders and, like all Iranians, had a penchant for dominating their peers. The surprising part was that unlike the bigoted Arabs, the businessmen of the erstwhile era spoke fluent Urdu, a language that both Indians and Pakistanis can follow clearly. The Galadaris had completed their initial schooling from Karachi's St Patrick's High School, which is why they were fluent in Urdu as well in addition to their expertise in Arabic, Persian and English.

Khalid spoke with enthusiasm but did not overdo his pitch. The Galadaris were impressed with this young twenty-four-year-old man from India. Abdul Wahab felt he had a lot of promise.

Until then, the Galadaris had been dealing with a cartel of well-known Pakistani smugglers, including Haji Ashraf. These smugglers had monopolized the gold market in Dubai and the Indians were left with negligible representation. 'With your help, Pakistani businessmen have minted money so much so that they boast of gold doors and silver walls. All I am asking for is one chance to prove myself,' Khalid had said with the utmost earnestness in his voice.

Khalid's proposal was that all the future gold that Wahab and his brothers would smuggle to India would be through Khalid. That he would have the sole, exclusive right to Galadari's gold in Bombay. Wahab looked at his brothers Latif and Rahim, who both shrugged, indicating they needed to tread with caution; they could not afford to be reckless.

'How will you bypass the government? Even we could not do it and landed up on their wanted list,' Wahab said, trying to penetrate Khalid's defences.

Khalid rose from the sofa. He looked imposing, towering at 6 feet 2 inches. He wanted to add emphasis to what he was about to say. 'It is the government's job to be strict as they have to run the administration. But we have our own skills. *Hum bhooke sher ke moonh se gosht ka tukda nikal lete hain* (We have been known to steal a piece of flesh from the jaws of a hungry tiger),' Khalid said with aplomb, accentuating every single word in Urdu.

Wahab smiled, repeating every word, full of admiration for Khalid's chutzpah.

This dramatic line clinched the deal for Khalid. Wahab made his decision. He was always a risk-taker. He decided to stake his money on Khalid.

Wahab believed an alliance with Khalid for smuggling gold could work. He also convinced his brothers Rahim and Latif about the same. They shook hands, sealing a long-lasting partnership.

It has been forty-five years since Khalid's first meeting with Abdul Wahab, but he still remembers every single—though seemingly insignificant—detail. He cherishes the cordiality of the Galadari brothers in that first encounter, despite the fact that he was a rank newcomer. They eventually went on to establish a very strong bond that changed the fortunes for the Galadaris and Khalid and, later, Dawood Ibrahim.

But back then, when Khalid stepped out of their palatial beachside villa, he could not believe his good fortune. He had managed to swing the deal. Khalid had learnt from experience that if something was meant to happen, it would happen, come what may. And if things didn't happen smoothly and the path seemed littered with obstacles, then it was never meant to be. He felt the meeting with the Galadari brothers was a good omen.

When he had landed in Dubai, Khalid was given the impression that the Galadari brothers were the Big Daddies of Dubai when it came to gold smuggling and that the local Watnis were not happy with their clout and popularity. He was not at all sure whether he would even manage to gain an audience with them, let alone walk away with a lucrative smuggling deal.

Khalid, of course, was not aware that it was Abdul Wahab who had won the round. In one of his dhow trips to the Bombay coast, he got arrested by DRI sleuths. However, he had managed to secure bail from the court and escaped to Dubai. The DRI could not believe that Abdul Wahab had hoodwinked them and slipped away so easily. He was declared wanted in India. Subsequently, both his brothers too were declared proclaimed offenders by the Indian government.

After the lookout notice was issued for Abdul Wahab, he was in search of somebody reliable for his gold-smuggling operations in India, when Khalid landed at his doorstep. With Khalid monitoring the whole operation from the Dubai coast to Bombay's landing spots, Abdul Wahab was sure to have a huge load lifted off his shoulders. The trust factor was not an issue at all. As the saying goes in the Mumbai mafia, '*Beimani ke saare dhande imaandaari se hote hain* (All dishonest businesses are executed with the utmost honesty).'

After concluding the meeting, Khalid did not stay back in Dubai for any sightseeing, despite it being his first trip abroad. Instead, he rushed back home to execute his smuggling plans.

When he landed in India, he rushed to Teli Mohalla and narrated the whole story to Bashu. 'And that is how I clinched the deal. Now we will be numero uno in the smuggling business.'

Bashu did not react but gave him an enigmatic smile.

The windfall happened in a very short span of time. Khalid handled a couple of gold consignments and, lo and behold, Bashu and Khalid's coffers were overflowing. And the Bashu gang suddenly catapulted to the top of the mafia hierarchy.

Haji Mastan and Yusuf Patel of Bombay, Sukur Narayan Bakhia of Gujarat and other big smugglers were shocked by the sudden success of the Bashu–Khalid gang.

In fact, according to a retired customs officer, Khalid was the first bona fide smuggler with properly monitored operations, which he supervised from coast to coast and vessel to vessel. Every step of the way—right from the Dubai port to the steamer in international waters, to the fishermen's boat and all the way to Bombay Harbour—was meticulously planned and executed. In the process all the other smugglers and rivals became reduced to landing agents. Everyone wished for a deputy like Khalid, who could take their business to the next level.

Khalid himself was on cloud nine. Not only was the gold smuggling happening smoothly, the financial transactions overseas as well as with the local Marwari businessmen and jewellers were also all happening without any hiccups.

The only bump in the road came from unexpected quarters. His boss, Bashu, who should have been celebrating their success and rewarding him for being an asset, was behaving in a mystifying manner. Khalid could not understand Bashu's annoyance with him. Lately, Bashu had also started shunning his company. He became fretful and their relations seemed to sour.

The truth was that Bashu was burning with jealousy and this had crippled his mind. He failed to appreciate his best asset and instead was beset with insecurities. His main apprehension was that Khalid would eventually topple him and take over his gang. He began to plan Khalid's downfall, or, as the mafia chroniclers would surmise, his own.

12

Forging a Bond

Rashid Taxi was running for his life. Pushing and shoving the passers-by, colliding with bicycle riders and oncoming scooters. He was trying to get away from Khalid, who was looming large over him like an angel of death. But Rashid was scrawny and lean, he could run faster. Khalid was heavier and had to strain harder to continue running behind Rashid.

Khalid had spotted Rashid near Chowki Mohalla. His first instinct was to rush towards him on a motorbike, but a quick glance at Maulana Shaukat Ali Road—one of the most congested roads in the south Mumbai area, leading from V.P. Road to Dongri—told him the plan would be futile. Khalid decided his feet would carry him faster than any vehicle. He signalled to his boys to accompany him. 'We have to confront Rashid today,' he announced even as he picked up speed.

People stared, wide-eyed, at the chase. Khalid and his two boys were pushing, jumping and sometimes leaping because the road was always chock-a-block with obstacles. Too many people, too many footpath kiosks, too many hawkers, too many vehicles parked illegally on the roads, too many handcarts and too many honking vehicles—all in all, a picture of perpetual chaos. Both Khalid and Rashid were familiar faces in the area, so the locals who recognized them simply made themselves scarce in awe and fear, dreading major violence. They did not want to be caught in the crosshairs of this high-octane action. Some shop owners had hastily downed their shutters, lest one of the participants enter the shop and inadvertently cause irrevocable financial loss.

At one point of time, Khalid felt that Rashid was slipping away—he didn't even want to imagine the repercussions of such a possibility. His name would be dragged through the mud and Rashid would become emboldened enough to cock a snook at him. The chase ending successfully was very important for Khalid. He not only wanted to discipline Rashid but also terminate the possibility of any more Rashids rearing their ugly heads and threatening Bashu in the future.

Bashu's arrogance had spawned a legion of detractors in the area. His financial growth and Khalid's increasing clout had become a headache for several people in the neighbourhood. Bashu expected everyone to pay obeisance to him. If anybody failed to be subservient, the poor fellow was a marked man. One of them was a Muslim League member of the Legislative Assembly called Ziauddin Bukhari, a political leader with considerable influence. When Bukhari refused to do Bashu's bidding, the haughty ganglord engineered his defeat in the subsequent elections. One diktat from Bashu was enough to frighten people into doing his bidding. No, it was not respect that Bashu garnered, but fear. Bashu fed off people's fear and grew more powerful.

A Sufi saint by the name of Nirale Shah Baba was highly venerated among the Muslims of the area. This was an era when Wahabism had yet to take root among the Muslims of Dongri and Sufi saints were not taboo. Nirale Shah sat outside the Makhdoomiya Bakery across the road from Teli Mohalla. His presence attracted a sizeable crowd of devotees, a fact that angered Bashu. Nobody else in his fiefdom was allowed to attract a fan following larger than his—most definitely not a maverick old man with no money. He felt the Baba had the potential to dilute his power centre. Bashu's men often chided the baba for the milling crowds. They also asked him to meet with Bashu. But Nirale Shah Baba did not pay any heed to them as he felt it was beneath his dignity to kowtow to a local strongman.

Bashu finally sent a couple of toughies to Nirale Shah's *maghrib* (evening) prayer gatherings to rough up the devotees and shoo them away. The dispersed followers were hurt and humiliated, but who could argue with goons.

Finally, one fine day, Ziauddin Bukhari, along with Nirale Shah's devotees, cobbled together a convenient alliance to put the fear of God into Bashu. They held clandestine meetings in the area, and sometimes even in a different area, so that Bashu and Khalid did not get a whiff of their plans.

After the secret brainstorming sessions, the consensus was that only a parallel force equally driven and strong, could outwit Bashu and undermine his growing power. The anti-Bashu coterie assembled a ragtag band of young men and formed an *anjuman* (a group) and called themselves the 'Young Company'. Bukhari, in a clever, strategic move, also roped in Ibrahim Havildar and convinced him to give his blessings to their organization. However, Ibrahim Havildar was shrewdly kept in the dark about the real motive for the creation of this band of youths. He was persuaded to help with the ostensible purpose of constructively channelizing the energies of the wayward youths of Dongri. (The formation, strategic plans and eventual degeneration of the Young Company into a criminal cartel has been elaborated in *Dongri to Dubai*.)

Rashid Khan was popularly known as Rashid Taxi as he owned a fleet of black-and-yellow taxis. The mafia identifies people with the same name by adding a sobriquet to distinguish one from the rest. Rashid Taxi had a history with Bashu. He had initially started off as a Bashu acolyte but left bitterly after being mistreated.

When those opposing Bashu formed the Young Company, they anointed Rashid at the helm. Rashid, in his new-found status, perceived himself to be the director of the Young Company. He became exactly what he hated about Bashu. He began flexing his muscles, behaving insolently in the area, at times slapping Bashu's men at the slightest pretext or even abusing Bashu in public, behind his back, of course. Both Bashu and Khalid were reluctant to directly take on the Young Company as Ibrahim Bhai was involved. Ibrahim Havildar had connections in the police. It would have meant an open declaration of war in the area. Khalid had also genuinely liked Ibrahim Havildar and was not ready to do anything to offend him.

The discreet way of taking on the burgeoning role of the Young Company was by confronting Rashid and warning him off. Khalid, being Bashu's enforcer, called Rashid a couple of times through an emissary. But Rashid not only shrugged them off but also slapped and abused the messengers every time he was summoned. He told them, 'I don't have to submit to Bashu and his commands.'

For Khalid, it was a direct challenge. He finally decided to discipline Rashid in his own way. There is a proverb in the mafia circles, '*Pehelwan khopdi, puri chokdi* (A wrestler's brain only wants to wreck completely).' He alerted his men and posted a couple of boys at the end of Teli Mohalla; if they spotted Rashid passing by that route, they were to alert him immediately.

That evening in the summer of 1973, Khalid's boys told him about Rashid's presence in the area. Khalid swung into action immediately. Two of those boys who were earlier beaten by Rashid also joined the chase. They knew that Khalid not only wanted to shatter Rashid's pride but also his bones. They were also itching to avenge their own humiliation at Rashid's hands.

After chasing Rashid for half a kilometre, Khalid, a heavyset man, had begun to pant, beads of sweat dotting his forehead. It was too much work for one day. Khalid feared that he would lose Rashid as the latter had begun to gain ground. This is exactly what Khalid was afraid of—that Rashid would disappear from sight and melt into the crowd. This was Khalid's final chance. If he lost Rashid today, he was afraid Rashid would become more alert thereafter and become as elusive as an eel. He would also mock him behind his back and, worse, Khalid would face embarrassment in front of his boss, Bashu.

Since the time Khalid had started working for Bashu, he had never ever failed in any assignment. It seemed that today was not his day and he would have to return to his den, shamed and defeated. Khalid had begun to slow down. His back was aching, his knees were feeling heavy and his feet felt like lead. He was breathing hard and his heart was thumping loudly. It is said that heavy, muscular man do not make good runners because their muscles and the inflexible weight of their bodies become an impediment. In contrast, lean and lightweight men have an edge over them. Wrestlers do not enjoy running. Except for swimming, they are not trained to undertake any aerobic activity.

Khalid was thoroughly frustrated at such a potential loss of face and decided to give up. Both his men who were running behind him were also out of breath. They stopped the moment they saw Khalid slowing down. They decided to return and were resigned to their fate.

Suddenly, like a bolt from the blue, a youth whizzed past them, almost flying with extreme agility, jumping across the handcarts, hopping away in front of the honking car bonnets, intercepting motorbikes and scooters. Khalid turned to look in wonderment, surprised at the sudden surge of energy that one of his boys seemed to have acquired in no time. But as he turned around, he saw both his men were still behind him, the epitome of deflated tyres, thoroughly punctured. They too looked at him incomprehensibly and shrugged, acknowledging that they too didn't know who this man was, sprinting ahead of them like a rabbit.

It was obvious by now that the teenager was on their side, as he seemed to be in hot pursuit of Rashid Taxi. Khalid's aching heels suddenly sprung to life. The young boy had revived his hopes. He began jogging to check if the young man had been able to accomplish what he could not do. And lo and behold, Khalid was pleasantly surprised to see that the galloping boy had caught up with Rashid near Peerkhan Street no. 1 and was calling for him to take over. The youth was holding Rashid Taxi by his collar and was not allowing him to move an inch from the spot.

'*Khalid Bhai, aa jao* (Come here, Khalid Bhai),' said the boy.

While Khalid was overjoyed that Rashid had finally been cornered, he looked quizzically at the boy who held Rashid in his firm grip. One of his aides announced, 'Yeh to Dawood hai (Oh, this is Dawood).'

Khalid was trying hard to size up this scrawny lad who had been introduced to him by Ibrahim Havildar just recently, and who was now holding Rashid like a sack of potatoes, with so little effort. Khalid patted Dawood's back, indicating that he was very pleased with his actions. The boy had no idea that Rashid was a prize catch for Khalid and by netting him he had rescued him from a tight spot.

Then Khalid turned swiftly and administered a resounding, heavy slap—in full force—on Rashid's face. Rashid collapsed to the ground, his lips bleeding.

Rashid's arrogance and belligerence, added with his audacious near-escape, had enraged Khalid. He wanted to kill him—crush him and smother him to death. But so far there had been no police complaints against Khalid and he did not want to start now. Killing Rashid in full public view with so many witnesses would definitely result in his conviction.

But Khalid was determined to punish him and make a lesson out of him to serve as a deterrent for others who dared snub Bashu. In the few years that he had been with the Mumbai mafia, he had learnt the golden rules too well. If you want to kill someone, then you stab him in the stomach. But if you want him to live but still want to subject him to abject and disgraceful humiliation, then you stab him in his buttocks.

This is called *'gaand pe waar'*—attack on the arse. The injury inflicted in full public view would be a perennial source of embarrassment for the victim and he would never be able to sit straight even after recovery. Eventually, among Bombay denizens, this form of retribution got whittled down to *'gaand pe laat'* (kick on the arse) and, now, GPL is a widely used acronym.

Khalid took a knife from his aide and drove the knife down both of Rashid's butt cheeks, leaving two deep gashes. Rashid let out a piercing scream. Khalid and his men were satisfied with the punishment and were ready to leave. It was then that one of his men asked, '*Bhai, agar police case hua toh?* (Bhai, what if the police registers a case against us?)'

This question stopped Khalid in his tracks. He had been preparing to gloat to Bashu about Rashid's public chastisement at his hands. According to Indian penal laws, an assault could still be interpreted under Section 307 (attempt to murder) of the IPC, or even under Section 326 (voluntarily causing grievous hurt by dangerous weapons or means).

Dawood, who was, until now, merely standing by without participating in the violence, stepped forward and said, 'If there is a cross complaint of a similar case, then the police will resolve it within the station premises and the matter will not go to court, thereby ruling out any prosecution or trial.' Dawood had simplified their dilemma and spoken like a true policeman's son.

Khalid's brow creased in worry, 'How can we lodge a cross complaint against Rashid when we don't have a victim whom he has hurt?' Khalid inquired from Dawood and also looked towards his two men.

Even before Khalid's aides could respond, Dawood acted with the same swiftness that he had displayed earlier while chasing Rashid. He took the knife from Khalid and inflicted a deep gash on his own forearm. Fresh hot blood gushed out from his wound and splattered on his clothes, and also began dribbling on the tar road. Dawood's clothes were soaked with his own blood. Everything happened so suddenly and abruptly that Khalid was left stunned at Dawood's initiative and even sacrifice.

The day Dawood shed his own blood was the day he conquered Khalid's heart. The boy was ten years his junior but was so quick on the uptake. He had saved him from a legal complication and had also plucked Rashid like a ripe fruit in no time, that too when he was not even a stakeholder. It was at that precise moment that he vowed to himself that he would stand by the young man and protect him always, even if he had to give up his own life to save him.

Khalid immediately gave Dawood a warm, crushing embrace and asked his men to tie a bandage on Dawood's forearm. He then personally rushed him to the state-run J.J. Hospital's casualty ward, which was just across the road.

It was the beginning of a long-lasting bond.

13

Survival Techniques

The sharp knife in Dawood's hand moved with amazing swiftness, grazing Khalid's left triceps. Khalid's timely defence had saved him by a whisker. The knife's sharp point had managed to tear into his T-shirt sleeve, causing a scratch. Instead of showing anger or irritation, Khalid looked at Dawood with admiration and approval.

'*Bahut khoob, Dawood, tum bahut jaldi seekh gaye* (Very well done, Dawood, you have learnt very quickly).'

It was barely the fifth day since Dawood had begun training with Khalid, but his protégé was already surpassing the mentor's expectations. Khalid was impressed because, as he recalled, he himself had taken quite a while to master the knife despite having a good teacher like Bashu. He was a man of strength and believed that unless he had a strong grip of the weapon, his learning was superficial. Khalid took several weeks to master the forward and reverse grips of the knife, eventually settling for the forward grip.

'Real dexterity lies in holding the handle of the knife gingerly. If you do that, the position of the knife's edge can be changed as per the strategy of attack. A strong grip will impede the swift movement of the blade of the knife, by which time your adversary could have disarmed you or managed to inflict injury,' lectured Khalid.

Even before Khalid had begun Dawood's training, the latter was already adroit at handling switchblades. The switchblade is convenient to carry, and its main objective is to terrify the onlooker by the mere gesture of switching open the knife with one swift flick of the blade, held between the thumb and the forefingers of the right hand. The mechanical *krrrrr* sound and the erect bare knife were enough to instil fear even in the minds of the onlookers. Even hardened gangsters who carried the switchblade were prone to being wary of this harm-inflicting knife.

In Bollywood, actor Shatrughan Sinha, who often played a street ruffian, wielded the switchblade, or Rampuri *chaku,* in a particular style that embodied machismo. His fans would burst into applause and whistles the moment he brandished his Rampuri chaku, turning his face in a particular way even while slaying his opponent with his 'dialogues', a very generic, broad term in the Hindi-film industry. It can include abuses, war of words, interesting conversation, diatribe and everything else that pertains to an interesting exchange of words.

Once Dawood mastered the art of knife fighting, Khalid began imparting lessons on unarmed close combat. The idea was to fight and defeat a group of thugs, if cornered, single-handedly. Khalid referred to it as 'survival technique', while Dawood called it a 'hero fight'.

'Since you don't have much body mass, the only asset that you do have in your arsenal is your agility and nimble movement, which heavyset or big people normally don't have,'

Khalid Pehelwan (centre) on his wedding day,
flanked by Anees on his right and Dawood on his left.

Khalid Pehelwan (left) chilling out with
Dawood Ibrahim after his nikah (right).

Khalid Pehelwan (close-up).

Khalid Pehelwan (centre) with Dawood Ibrahim on his right and Dawood's brother Noor Hasan, also called 'Noora', on his left.

Khalid Pehelwan with mafia queen Jenabai Daruwali.

Khalid Pehelwan (left) with Dawood Ibrahim and the baap of dons—former head constable Ibrahim Kaskar.

Khalid Pehelwan in his college days, doing his drill for the National Cadet Corps.

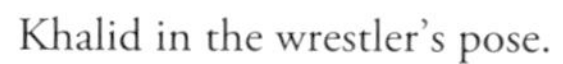

Khalid in the wrestler's pose.

Togetherness: Khalid (left) and Dawood (right).

Another picture of Khalid (left) and Dawood (right).

A photograph of Khalid from fairly recent times.

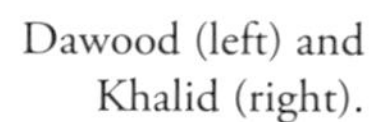

Dawood (left) and Khalid (right).

A photograph from Khalid's NCC training days.

A photograph from Khalid's NCC training days.

A photograph from Khalid's NCC training days.

Khalid told Dawood. 'What would you do if you are faced with a man like me? He could easily crush you with his strength.'

Despite Dawood being in awe of Khalid, he shot back, '*Nahin, bhai, aapko challenge nahin karoonga, lekin mai bhi halwa nahin hoon* (No, brother, I will not dare to challenge you, but rest assured, when push comes to shove, I will be no cakewalk).'

Khalid nodded. The boy's aplomb never ceased to amaze him. He taught him many things.

One of them was how to break the crushing embrace of an adversary, if held tightly from behind. 'You have to smash the adversary's nose with a head butt, or stomp with full strength on the enemy's big toe. And if nothing else works, try to find some room and pull your back away from him, bend your knees and throw him off your back, commonly known as *"dhobi pachad"* [a washerman's throw] in wrestling parlance.'

'If none of the above tricks work, then there is a fatal mantra that can kill by breaking the enemy's neck,' Khalid explained. 'The elbow is such an underestimated weapon in a man's body. One perfect full-throttle elbow assault, heaved from chest height and hit below the opponent's chin, can throw even King Kong off his foot. Chances are that it may snap the neck bone if the right amount of power is used in the attack.'

Khalid continued his lessons excitedly: 'Even the strongest man cannot take a hit on the knee joint, it can topple him. Again, the right amount of force is needed and it should connect at the most sensitive point. In desperate situations, always go for smaller body parts which are the most vulnerable for a man. Like sticking your fingers in the nostrils forcibly, pulling the earlobes, gouging the eyes out and, if you happen to be below the waist level and your hands cannot reach the face, then try squeezing the testicles tightly. All this will cause an immeasurable amount of agony to your enemy and he will let go of you.'

Dawood was Khalid's first sincere pupil ever since he had left his home town of Harda in Madhya Pradesh. He liked that Dawood was absorbing everything he said, like a sponge. He knew the boy held great promise. He possessed a fire and drive rarely seen in other boys of his age.

Dawood was savouring and relishing the lessons. For the lanky, scrawny Dawood, this was a dream come true. He always wanted to be a real toughie. He wanted to be invincible, a boy who could fend off several opponents in one go.

Whenever he was not playing cricket in the precincts of J.J. Hospital or loafing around with the boys on the streets or scamming people through his '*palti marna* technique' (replacing a watch with a dud), he was hooking up with Khalid for more lessons. Khalid often called Dawood to Bashu's wrestling pit for training. When Dawood's friends, envious of his new-found abilities, also wanted to learn the tricks of the trade and sought Khalid out, the teacher politely ignored their overtures.

Khalid was very rooted in reality. He was educated but had no airs about him. He never made a big deal of his strength unless so demanded by the occasion. He would plonk himself on a charpoy right on the street and order food from the nearby joints. He would not hesitate to ask hangers-on to share his meals with him right. He had no qualms about wearing a lungi. He was equally comfortable in bell-bottoms, a lungi or a Pathani suit. He never wanted to imitate film stars and he never wanted to impress anybody. The man was a pehelwan to the core. The flashy world and its trappings were not for him.

While Dawood relied on Khalid for his leadership skills, fighting techniques and, later in life, to learn the tricks of the smuggling business, his reference point for the material things was not Khalid. While his teacher was a heroic strongman who trained him in self-defence, Dawood drew inspiration for power play and money, clothes and style from other places. Bashu, for instance, who always smoked the most expensive cigarette of his time, 555, flaunted a lighter made of pure gold, and was always bedecked in a pristine white shirt, white pants and white shoes. The mafia bosses in Bombay, like the politicians, only wore white.

Haji Mastan and Karim Lala loved the white shirt and white trousers. They claimed that they were following the Islamic tradition of wearing whites, but even Varadarajan Mudaliar wore a white shirt and white *veshti* (lungi) at all times.

As if not content with the white dress code, the mafia dons thought it fit to complement it with customized white leather shoes. Over the years, the mafia dress code has undergone several transformations but the white shoe is still in vogue. The rich and nouveau rich in Pydhonie, Dongri and the J.J. area, or even in the Middle Eastern countries, can still be seen flaunting their white footwear. Wearing white shoes brings luck, it is believed.

Despite Dawood's tendency to veer towards the flashy, Khalid was indulgent of him. He had seen the boy emerge out of his cocoon. After all, the boy was from a different generation. He had also developed a liking for him since Rashid Taxi's butt-stabbing incident. Rashid had tried to lodge an FIR against Khalid at the Dongri police station, which was immediately countered by Dawood's FIR of an equally serious and rather exaggerated complaint against Rashid.

The Dongri police convinced Rashid to withdraw his complaint, else they would have to take cognizance of Dawood's allegations too. Since Dawood was also the son of a policeman, the scales would be tipped in his favour, they said. Rashid was forced to withdraw his complaint against Khalid.

To add insult to injury, Dawood also influenced the Young Party against Rashid. In no time, Dawood had replaced Rashid as the Young Party chief. Khalid was really happy with Dawood's handiwork and smart machinations.

Khalid's boss, Bashu, should have been happy at the turn of events. His man Friday had snipped a growing threat in the bud, in the form of the Young Party, and neutralized it by placing an insider like Dawood at the helm. Bashu's turf was intact but Bashu's feelings were not. There was something about Dawood that made him uneasy. The boy was very intelligent, and his eyes had a sparkle, a mischievous look that said, 'Hold it right there, I will take your place soon.'

Bashu had also not liked the promotion of Dawood as the leader of the Young Party and he also vehemently disapproved of the growing friendship between Khalid and Dawood. But in either case, he realized he could not intervene. Bashu could neither influence Dawood's appointment as the leader of the Young Party because the weight of Ibrahim Havildar's clout and reputation was behind his son, coupled with the fact that the group had been ostensibly formed with the intention of giving a constructive direction to the youth, and nor could he ask Khalid to sever his ties with Dawood. He knew Khalid was obliged to the young boy who had saved him from a police case, and their friendship meant that the Young Party would not bay for his blood. But much as he tried, the uneasiness did not leave Bashu.

He was waiting for an opportune moment to either get rid of them or break up their friendship.

Heedless of the tumult in Bashu's mind, Khalid and Dawood went about their lives without the slightest inkling as to what the future had in store for them. They were under the assumption that like so many people who cross your paths at a certain stage and disappear, never to be seen or heard from again, they too would soon outgrow each other's company. Their association and bond was born out of a need from one side and an obligation from the other. They presumed they would go their separate ways with the passage of time. At no point of time did either of them feel that they would be shaping each other's destiny or forging a bond that would last almost a lifetime.

14

The Mafia in the 1970s

There are times in life when you feel absolutely at one with yourself. Khalid felt a deep sense of well-being, as if he had managed to draw out all that life had to offer from the well of the universe. After establishing a well-oiled gold-smuggling mechanism, his life seemed to have found a purpose. Minor irritants like Hassu Maharaj and the budding menace of the Young Party had been duly neutralized. His burgeoning bank balance made him immensely happy and he shared his new-found wealth with his mother and other relatives who needed to be taken care of. Somewhere in the far recesses of his mind, though, there was a buried dream of donning a police uniform. But he would deliberately pull himself back to find solace in the wads of banknotes and all the gold he owned.

In keeping with this fresh status, he moved away from the mafia capital of Dongri, its various labyrinthine mohallas and rented out a plush flat in Bombay Central, which was much more upmarket than Dongri. Bombay Central was less congested and had bigger homes. The areas of Dongri, Pydhonie, J.J. Market, Umarkhadi—popularly known as

'3, 8 and 9' (Bombay pincode numbers)—had back-to-back buildings that shared walls, with poor hygiene and no civic amenities. Almost all the monotonously built buildings had dank corridors, narrow wooden creaking stairs, common toilets and the all-pervasive stench of rotten garbage that was dumped in the common enclosed yard of the building. The lack of physical space had also impinged on the mind space of the gangsters, who had never thought bigger.

In the 1970s, the Bombay mafia's ambitions were not far-reaching and were yet to take proper shape. Their fiefdom began and ended with their lanes and adjacent lanes and some intersections. The J.J. Hospital intersection, which is not a huge or expansive area, had several by-lanes and mohallas. Interestingly, every by-lane had a dada whose writ ran large in the area. Bashu Dada ruled the roost in Teli Mohalla, where he had his gym, *baithak* (gathering place) and his residence. Dawood Ibrahim's father, Ibrahim Havildar, too had a house in this small, narrow lane and Dawood was born in one such cramped house measuring barely 100 sq. ft. That's how Ibrahim Bhai and Bashu Dada knew each other and were apparently friends. The Kaskar clan later moved to Temkar Mohalla, which is adjacent to Teli Mohalla.

Hassu Maharaj threw his weight around in Khanda Mohalla, which was also known as Hujra Mohalla. Then there was Chowki Mohalla, so called because of a police chowki at the end of the street; this was unclaimed territory.

A little further away was Siddhi Mohalla, which housed over 2000 families belonging to an ethnic African race. They made India their home for 500 years ago when the Portuguese brought them here as slaves. They are Sufi Muslims. The leader of the Siddhis, as this tribe is called, was a local toughie called Kareem Siddhi, a lookalike of the Ugandan despot Idi

Amin—and he was referred to by this name by the local cops and everybody else. Those were the days when Idi Amin's atrocities against his own people was in the news. Kareem Siddhi, of course, loved the moniker and began dressing up in military uniform to keep up the facade.

Every Friday, after the Jumma prayers, Kareem Siddhi used to don the military uniform with his black shades, trying to look every inch like Idi Amin. And then he would stand on a platform and give fiery speeches to an audience comprised mainly of his acolytes and some of his community members. The common Siddhis raised their hands to hail him and encouraged him the way the Nazis raised their hands to support the leader of the Third Reich, Adolf Hitler. As long as Kareem Siddhi was alive, no gangster, mafia don or policeman dared to cross swords with him. The Idi Amin of Mumbai ruled in his small fiefdom unchallenged. The Siddhis were never attracted to radical Islam by the Salafis or the Tablighis, who were gradually making inroads into Dongri. The Siddhis remained liberal Sufi followers and adhered to the discipline staunchly. They subsequently set up dargahs of Sufi saints in the area. After Kareem Siddhi's death, there were no more Idi Amins. Slowly the Siddhi population too migrated to Arab countries for greener pastures. Presently there are barely fifty Siddhi families residing in Siddhi Mohalla. They stayed behind to keep company with their patron saint.

Beyond the Siddhi Mohalla was Jail Road South, considered to be the stronghold of Abdul Rahim Khan and his sons, while his brother Abdul Karim Khan, alias Karim Lala, ruled the Grant Road area of Baida Gully. Karim Lala also called the shots in his brother's area and vice versa.

Beyond Grant Road and Novelty Cinema was Bombay's red-light area, comprising Kamathipura, Foras Road and

Playhouse, mispronounced as 'Pila House'. These areas were ruled by a local dada called Shahid, who had his baithak in Arab Galli.

In fact, the gangs had few means of relieving people of their hard-earned money. The red-light area had only two kinds of income for the underworld dadas. The most despicable source of making money was living off the income earned through the physical exploitation of women who were forced into prostitution. It worked through the local network of prostitutes, marketed by pimps and the *gharwali* (the brothel's female manager) who had reached her position after growing old and spending decades in the flesh trade. The gharwalis and pimps collected cash in the morning from the helpless prostitutes and gave it to Haji Umar, who was the head of all the pimps and was pejoratively referred to as 'Bhadvon ka Boss', meaning the 'chief of pimps'. Umar used to make thousands of rupees every night, and would keep bringing girls from the northern and southern Indian states as per the demand. At the time, Umar ruled the red-light area with an iron fist. Not much is known about Umar except that his mother, Ayesha, was a ragpicker-turned-sex worker. Ayesha had turned out to be quite popular in the area and lived with a local pimp who supplied girls to top politicians in the state. Umar had been brought up by the pimp, who had promoted him to take charge of the Kamathipura area. Umar was also a homosexual and often sodomized his own sex workers before inducting them in the trade.

Within these *pinjaras* (birdcages) and red-light-area lanes were a series of seedy cinemas, which included Taj Talkies, Shalimar, Nishad, Super Talkies and Royal Talkies. Those were the days when movie tickets were sold in advance and people stood in serpentine queues to get tickets for the advance show of their favourite matinee idol. At times, when a film was considered a blockbuster, people would stand in a queue for over forty-eight hours to get tickets through advance booking. The prices were steep but tickets were readily bought by those willing to pay for it. It was the time when the blockbuster *Bobby* was released, marking Dimple Kapadia's debut, at the beginning of 1973, which was followed by Amitabh Bachchan's watershed movie *Zanjeer*, released a few months after *Bobby*. However, Dimple's bikini act in *Bobby* drew a far bigger crowd than Jaya Bhaduri's well-draped character in *Zanjeer*. There were endless queues for *Bobby*, which remained unabated for months.

Shahid of Arab Galli saw an opportunity in these huge queues and invented the '*chaar* anna scheme'. If someone was in queue and wanted to jump his position and progress by ten people ahead of him, then he would have to shell out chaar anna (25 paise). Similarly, if he wanted to bypass 100 other people before him, he would have to shell out Rs 2.50, which was the cost of a movie ticket in those days. Incidentally, the Bachchan starrer *Zanjeer* did not have as many chaar-anna takers.

Umar did not like Shahid encroaching on his turf and making money through just any means. He wanted to muscle him out, but Karim Lala, who lived next door, intervened and publicly humiliated the pimp. '*O Umar harami ka bachcha, tum bhadwagiri karo, usko phillum dekhne do* (O you bastard Umar, you focus on pimping; let Shahid watch movies).' Umar was infuriated by this and could not defy Karim Khan, who was the biggest muscle in those days and had the financial support of Haji Mastan and an ally in Varadarajan Mudaliar. Since Mastan and the other Muslim dons in the area sought respectability by making a religious pilgrimage to the holy city of Mecca and thus used the prefix of Haji before their names (Haji Mastan), Umar too followed suit and decided to rechristen himself as Haji Umar, so that people would stop referring to him as 'Bhadwa Umar' or 'Bhadve Ki Aulad' ('Umar the pimp' or 'son of a pimp').

Shahid was emboldened by Karim Lala's support and devised a new way of mocking Umar, not to mention making a quick buck. The debauched Arabs from Saudi Arabia had begun making business trips to Bombay. Shahid began supplying young girls to these Arabs in five-star hotels for Rs 1000. For a virgin, the price was Rs 5000. The trade was crudely christened as 'ribbon-cutting ceremony', a euphemism for deflowering virgins.

This business became quite popular with the Arabs and Shahid began making a lot of money. Umar watched helplessly as it was his trade, but since it was not conducted in his territory, he could not do anything. Shahid modified the trade and decided to sell the girls to these Arabs in the guise of marriage. He exploited the poverty of Indian Muslims and persuaded them to marry off their teenage girls to the Arab sheikhs in return for money that they desperately needed.

The Arabs were more than happy with this aspect of prostitution, seeing as they were able to get young virgin girls for a throwaway price of Rs 10,000. One could see sixty-year-olds marrying several twelve-year-olds. Shahid had also begun to import young girls from Hyderabad to sell them off to the Arabs. This went largely unnoticed by the government until the 1991 incident in which eleven-year-old Hyderabad resident Ameena Begum, who had been married off to an old Arab, was rescued by a courageous flight attendant Amrita Ahluwalia from an Indian Airlines flight. Despite the incident-making headlines, the business continued for a long time. Numerous such hoax marriages were conducted by pseudo *qazis* (priest) in the Dongri area until Umar decided that he had to take over the business from Shahid through some ruse.

Those who were not into the flesh trade or the black market decided to operate gambling dens (through *matka* gambling) but none could touch the business of bootlegging as Varadarajan had monopolized it so much that from Dharavi to Dahanu and on the central railway line until Dombivli, he had the sole authority to brew and distribute liquor.

Every turf was thus demarcated and restricted to a particular mafia group. Until the Pathan gang—led by Amirzada–Alamzeb, went on a rampage, opposed only by a twenty-year-old Dawood, who boasted a band of loyalists—none of the gangsters ever thought of consolidating their hold over the entire south Bombay area.

It was against this backdrop that Khalid aspired to think big and transact on gargantuan scales. Khalid laughed at the chaar-anna scheme and disapproved of the flesh trade. After moving on to gold smuggling from landing silver bricks, Khalid was ready to go to the next level—diamond smuggling.

While Khalid was happy with gold smuggling, he was in a mood to multiply his profits. He wanted something that would pose the least amount of trouble with the authorities and something with minimum complications. Gold could not be carried on flights as the vigilance therein was too much, whereas diamonds could be easily smuggled in through airports. Diamonds worth several lakhs could be easily kept in the pocket, hidden in the underwear or camouflaged in other accessories. The diamonds, depending on the number of carats and the cut, could make a minimum margin of over

200 per cent and could be easily sold in the Surat or Ahmedabad diamond markets, if not in Opera House or Zaveri Bazaar in Bombay.

Khalid threw the idea to Bashu, who was initially hesitant because of the bigger investment he would have to make and the consequent risks involved in the new business, but Khalid managed to convince him and left for Dubai.

Abdul Wahab Galadari was quite pleased with Khalid's dedication to the business and was quick to observe that so far they had not suffered any losses. He decided to give Khalid a chance with diamond smuggling. Galadari displayed an immense amount of implicit trust and handed him diamonds worth over Rs 3 lakh. This was also a litmus test for Khalid about whether he could evade the customs officers successfully and make a decent revenue from the diamonds.

Khalid was aware of the perils of the business. He decided to play smart and indulge in the systematic diversion of the authorities, as was the case with industrial espionage. Khalid carried a gold biscuit with him, stashed in the space meant for a camera roll. Those were the days when pictures were taken on a reel and not stored on a hard disk. To let the law enforcers notice the smaller folly, allow him to pay the fine after looking sorry and distract them from the bigger scam—this was the age-old tactic employed by all kinds of diamond smugglers and traders.

When Khalid reached Bombay, he hesitated and then walked towards a customs officer and declared that he was carrying a gold biscuit. The customs officer glared at him and then made him pay a duty of Rs 25,000 on it. The customs officer reprimanded him for carrying gold, which Khalid explained was for his would-be bride. Khalid was lightly frisked but no attention was paid to his shoes, in which the diamonds were hidden in the heels.

Normally, the whole airport episode and the diamond venture should have enthused Bashu. But when Khalid came back and triumphantly narrated the story to him, he only received a withered look. That was the last nail in the coffin of his friendship with Bashu.

15

The Bashu–Khalid Split

Several burly, dour, poker-faced men had surrounded the building from all sides. They were sturdy and strongly built men who seemed to mean business. That July morning, nobody in their right minds would have messed with them.

These grim-faced men did not have any weapons on them but they compensated for it with their menace. Curious onlookers maintained a safe distance lest they fell foul of them. A few policemen, sporting their trademark antique SLR .303 guns, were also scattered about. When the entire area was properly secured, one of the men, who clearly seemed to be in charge, summoned two hefty men and issued instructions to them. He asked them to go upstairs with a few uniformed policemen carrying weapons.

Time seemed to stand still for those holding fort downstairs around the building. They were alert and prepared for any showdown. Interminable seconds passed before the team that went upstairs returned and joined their teammates for a short conclave. From their animated discussion and the fact that they had returned empty-handed, the onlookers surmised that the poor sod whom they had gone to pick up had probably flown the coop.

A nervous Khalid stood unobtrusively in a corner opposite the building, watching with trepidation the developments unfolding in this Bombay Central building on the busy Bellasis Road in south Bombay. He realized that his habit of eating an early brunch had saved him from being a sitting duck for those who had come hunting for him. At the time, he was not aware that the men who had come for him were the sleuths of the DRI accompanied by a posse of policemen.

He thanked his stars for his habit of always playing it safe. He never discussed his habits, eating spots and the location of his house with anybody. His personal life and his idiosyncrasies were nobody's business.

Earlier the same day, around late morning, he had gone to a restaurant bang opposite his residence for a hearty breakfast of keema, tandoori roti and several eggs. As he was paying at the counter, the cashier, who knew him well, remarked, '*Aaj aapki building pe CID ki raid giri lagti hai* (Looks like the building you live in has been raided by the CID today).' Khalid's heartbeat quickened and his eyes reflected a momentary rush of fear. For a man who wanted to join the police force, being a fugitive on the run from the law did not come to him naturally. Playing hide-and-seek with the enforcement agencies had changed his psychology. But, of course, he was aware that since his foray into smuggling, he had crossed the Rubicon.

Before the cashier could catch his eyes again, Khalid had managed to quickly mask his emotions. He smiled and shrugged nonchalantly as he took the change. But once outside the restaurant, Khalid could not contain himself. He darted between groups of people to see the spectacle for himself.

Across the road, around Patel Mansion, where he lived on the first floor, the place was swarming with both plain-clothes and uniformed police officers.

How did the police discover him? Who squealed on him? He had kept his residence a closely guarded secret. Only a few from the inner sanctum knew his address. Bashu had come visiting only once. Khalid's life was not an open book; even though rival gangs had sniffed out his success, nobody knew his modus operandi.

Did he unwittingly cross swords with somebody that brought the police to his doorstep? Barring the Rashid Taxi–stabbing episode, which was summarily dismissed after Dawood's chicanery, Khalid was not involved in any serious offence.

The whole operation was seemingly called off after a brief discussion and the men had begun to disperse. However, Khalid was curious and his gaze began following the leader of the group, who walked towards a parked jeep and began talking to a man. The man that he was talking to came out of the jeep and stood next to him on the curb, smoking a cigarette. Khalid's heart fell to his stomach. The officer was talking to Bashu! Khalid was stunned. Was Bashu in league with the police and the CID? Did Bashu lead them to Khalid's house? Was he the snitch? The realization that Bashu had probably squealed on him hit Khalid with the force of an unstoppable steam engine. He staggered backwards in shock.

'Impossible. Impossible,' he kept muttering under his breath.

How did he miss this? Bashu's equation with him had never been the same since the time he had come back from Dubai after striking a deal with the Galadari brothers. Their relationship was further strained after Khalid received the green signal from the Galadari brothers for smuggling diamonds into India.

It had been very obtuse of Khalid to have missed the signs. Bashu had been very reserved with him for a while now. He had taken to replying in monosyllables and he seemed to be always preoccupied. He wouldn't meet Khalid's eyes during conversations, and when he did, they were expressionless. As he saw Bashu confabulating with the raiding party's leader that day, Khalid finally realized that another chapter in his life was over.

It had all started when a batch of diamonds sent by a diamond merchant from Bombay had been stolen. It was being transported through the unofficial courier network of boys called 'the Angadias', when they were robbed en route to Surat. A police complaint was filed by the diamond merchant. Incidentally, Bashu and Khalid also did business with the same diamond merchant. One thing led to another during the investigation and the police landed up at Bashu's door. Bashu realized that this was the best way to save himself and make Khalid the scapegoat. Bashu blamed the whole smuggling business on Khalid. India's premier anti-smuggling agency, the DRI, which is part of the Central excise and customs administration, also got involved and teamed up with the DRI to reach Khalid.

Around the same time, the DRI had seized unaccounted diamonds worth Rs 5 crore from an Angadia boy bound for Surat. The trail of investigation led the DRI to the diamond-market headquarters at Bombay's Opera House and subsequently to a mob boss from Dongri. They connected the diamonds seized from one Jignesh Dave of Radhesyam Angadia Services to Bashu Dada in Teli Mohalla.

The Angadias of Mumbai are a unique lot. They are men who work for diamond traders and jewellers and are generally very trustworthy. They wear a long *jhabba* with a pocket, while some prefer to carry a *jhola*. Diamonds worth millions of rupees are carried from Mumbai to Surat and elsewhere by these men. They look inconspicuous and blend in with the crowd. They are generally very reliable but not prone to conversations if you travel with them in trains, usually long-distance ones. They are known to be very discreet. Generally diamond and bullion traders from Bhuleshwar, Pydhonie, Kalbadevi, Dhobi Talao and Dalal Street in south Mumbai use them to transport important documents, gold, diamonds and wads of cash.

In the initial years, the Angadias used to transport legitimate diamonds, and later this unofficial route was appropriated as a channel for moving smuggled diamonds and unaccounted cash sent through the hawala route. They were never caught by the customs or the police. Recently, however, for the first time, Bombay customs officials had intercepted two Angadias while they were boarding a train to Surat after suspecting their role in smuggling diamonds.

Khalid decided to go underground for a couple of months until the pursuit got cold. But while in hiding, his unfinished business with Bashu kept niggling him. He couldn't sleep well, feeling restless all the time. One night he sneaked into Teli Mohalla to confront Bashu. He knew Bashu stayed awake until the wee hours of the night while the other residents slept. Khalid managed to walk into Bashu's baithak as he was surrounded by his acolytes.

Bashu's face was ashen, like he had spotted a ghost. He didn't expect Khalid to reappear so soon and walk into his lair.

Bashu was not only Khalid's first boss but also his benefactor. After meeting Bashu, Khalid had grown from strength to strength. He had become wealthy and enjoyed the comforts of life. He was hugely indebted to Bashu. In return, he was unswervingly loyal to Bashu. He had never raised his voice with him nor had he been impertinent. Though Khalid came to seek answers, he didn't breach the line. Khalid just stood transfixed in front of Bashu and looked at him for a long time without uttering a single syllable. Bashu was aware of Khalid's unflinching devotion and subservience. He had never anticipated such an awkward moment. After searching for his answers in Bashu's eyes for a long time, Khalid could only manage to utter with great effort:

'*Kyun* (Why)?'

Khalid had never questioned Bashu earlier. They had been working together for years by then. Often, Khalid's Hindu friends ribbed him, '*Bashu ka Hanuman.*' Khalid had then laughed it off and never taken offence. He had then taken it as a compliment. Khalid swallowed his bitterness and asked again: '*Kyun, Bashu Dada? Kyun kiya mere saath aisa?* (Why, Bashu Dada? Why did you do this to me?)'

Bashu took a long time to answer. He took a deep breath and said, 'The customs officer had reached my doorstep and wanted to make a smuggling case and needed an accused to be booked. I tried to ward them off initially but they began threatening to arrest me under COFEPOSA [the Conservation of Foreign Exchange and Prevention of Smuggling Activities Act]. It was either you or me.' It seemed to take an effort for Bashu to speak coherently.

'So you decided to make me the sacrificial lamb and protect yourself?' Khalid questioned him, his voice turning hoarse, eyes full of disappointment and hurt.

Bashu was finding it really difficult to convince Khalid. 'I felt that if they arrested me, then you would not be able to get me out while I would be able to get you out of jail in a jiffy with my contacts.'

Khalid was not willing to buy this warped logic of his supposedly omnipotent boss. The Bashu he knew had access to people in the police department, in the government and elsewhere. He could have easily protected Khalid from arrest, instead of leading them directly to his house.

'Bashu Dada, you could have offered any of your turds as a scapegoat for this purpose. Why did you snitch on me? Why throw your best man in the slammer? Why?' Khalid persisted.

He was now staring straight into Bashu's eyes, locking his gaze with him. Bashu looked away. One thought kept resonating in Khalid's mind: if Bashu could so easily crack under pressure and get the cops to arrest him, then he could also, as easily, get Khalid killed by his rivals without any qualms.

Bashu was unable to explain that he had actually become overcome by jealousy and felt insecure about his protégé's growing popularity and influence. Bashu could not honestly tell Khalid that he believed that a stint in jail would have made Khalid more humble and him happier.

The Bashu–Khalid saga of friendship and betrayal was so much like the legendary story of Antonio Salieri and Wolfgang Amadeus Mozart. Despite Salieri's seniority and clout, he became insecure of the much younger composer, Mozart. Finally, Salieri's jealousy and insecurity led him to plot the downfall of Mozart. In a similar vein, when Bashu got Khalid to Bombay, the boy was impressionable and raw. In the initial years he was just a muscleman. Bashu did not want Khalid to grow. Though he encouraged him, he thought he was indulging him. He didn't realize Khalid was more than just mere brawn.

After the gold-smuggling business picked up, Bashu realized Khalid's potential. But instead of channelizing Khalid's talent, he kept nursing his jealousy all the time. Khalid was young, Bashu was not. Khalid had a hunger for success and motivation to get ahead in life, and now he had the contacts too. Bashu was an ageing don with his circle of loyalists who were limited in their understanding of the world. Khalid was worldly-wise, and if he could manage to impress the Galadaris, who were very powerful at the time, it meant that he was no ordinary hanger-on gang member. Bashu did not want Khalid to topple him and take over the reins of the gang.

Old records were hard to find from the marine and preventive wings of the customs department, but an officer, who has long since retired, confided that it was indeed Ahmed Khan, alias Bashu Dada, who had facilitated the probe and promised cooperation in exchange for his own amnesty from prosecution. Khalid had been offered to them on a platter.

Feeling intensely drained, exhausted and heartbroken after his conversation with Bashu, Khalid walked away from Teli Mohalla, never to return to that street again. It would have been good for him if he could have just let off steam by beating the person who had caused him so much grief. But this was Bashu, the man he adored and protected.

That night, a great relationship and strong alliance was severed. Months passed and everybody forgot about the incident. But neither Khalid nor Bashu got over their wrenched parting. After Khalid's departure from the scene, Bashu's power and position was seriously undermined.

Khalid too suffered a major setback in his path. He could not go back to his village and become a recluse. He had placed loyalty over everything else in life, but Bombay had no place for such feelings. For a while he quit smuggling and disconnected from the mafia. He retreated into a shell. But money is the oxygen of life. Everyone has to make a living. Khalid could not mope around for long. He opened a social club in Bombay Central. 'Social Club' is a euphemism for a gambling den.

The club got him decent earnings and he began spending his time there.

Elsewhere, Dawood's star was on the rise. In a fortuitous turn of events, Dawood had been slowly building his resume in the mafia—he was inching up the ladder of notoriety and power among the mafia ranks. He had now grown into a strapping youth and was proficient in the art of self-defence, being able to use any weapon with felicity.

Considering the kind of rebellious youth that he had become, Dawood rarely respected anyone any more. But in the Bombay mafia, Dawood only respected his own elder brother, Sabir, and then Khalid, not necessarily in that order. Khalid was his first hero and mentor. Dawood had heard about Khalid's separation from Bashu, but he did not broach the topic with Khalid.

Dawood often visited Khalid at the club, their friendship continued and became stronger. Dawood also brought his brother Sabir and his other cronies to Khalid and they all hung out with him in the club through the night.

As time flew, Dawood crossed his teenage years and began causing havoc in the Dongri area along with his brother Sabir. Both the brothers were known for their high-handed behaviour. They were a menacing duo and were known to rough up those who failed to do their bidding. Their policeman father, Ibrahim Havildar, had long resigned himself to their ways.

Dawood had become very ambitious. He wanted to topple all the big daddies of crime and stake his claim for the numero uno position. Haji Mastan and Bashu Dada were the two most powerful dons at the time. Sabir and Dawood had witnessed their father's humiliation at the hands of the moneybags. Now that they were grown-ups, it was time to square up.

The first major crime that Dawood committed was a bank robbery on 4 December 1974. He thought he was plundering Mastan's money but it turned out to be cash that belonged to the Metropolitan Bank. But Dawood was not deterred. He kept chasing Mastan and his minions until the smuggler was finally upstaged; to counter this aggression, Mastan actually had to seek out Ibrahim Bhai and ask him to intervene by eating humble pie, by literally sitting on the floor while he was on the chair.

Bashu Dada was not so lucky, and Dawood was in no mood to forgive him. Besides, Dawood's mentor, Khalid, had left Bashu, so there was nobody who could stop him any more. Dawood attacked Bashu in such a way that the latter had to summon boys from his home town of Hyderabad to fend off Dawood. The boys turned out to be duds and were no match for Dawood's ferocity. He was a raging bull ready to trample anyone who crossed his path.

Dawood also smashed up Bashu Dada's gym and baithak in Teli Mohalla. The disgrace and insult suffered by the ruling don at the hands of a young boy was unbearable for him. Bashu Dada left the city overnight and migrated to Hyderabad.

After Bashu's exit, Dawood Ibrahim finally got the chance to reign supreme in his turf. There was only one obstacle in his path—the Pathan gang led by Amirzada and Alamzeb. He also longed to step into the world of smuggling.

Dawood was in a hurry to surmount the Pathans and realize his dreams.

16

The Art of Smuggling

Political iftars in the holy month of Ramadan are most exciting for those aspiring to climb the social ladder and others who want to do some serious networking. The grand feast after the fast is generally well attended by aspirational Muslims as well as non-Muslim politicians who want to make inroads into the community's vote bank.

It was during one such iftar that Ibrahim Havildar and A.R. Antulay were introduced to each other. Abdul Rehman Antulay was, at the time, a most sought-after politician in Maharashtra, despite the fact that he was a Muslim. He was a natural-born politician who knew the pulse of the masses. The public loved him as he was good with rhetoric. And he was a rising star. Antulay was also riding on a major streak of luck (that he could make inroads into the Maratha bastion in Maharashtra and live to tell the tale itself was no mean achievement). He also had a winning smile.

And, of course, the most important thing that swung the political dial in the right direction for him was that he was Indira Gandhi's favourite. When she appointed him as the minister for law and justice, Muslims felt it was a well-deserved appointment of a member of their own community, especially since Antulay had studied law. Grand felicitation functions were organized by the community for him. It seemed as though he would eventually weasel his way into the chief minister's throne itself given the way Mrs Gandhi was tilted towards him.

The grand iftar feast at the Anjuman-I-Islam school bang opposite the Victoria Terminus railway station was well attended by the community's prominent members. Antulay, of course, did not shake hands with Ibrahim Havildar. While they shared the same religion, hailed from the coastal belt of Konkan and were Konkani Muslims, they were separated by social hierarchy. Antulay was a barrister who had schooled in London while Ibrahim Havildar was a suspended cop trapped in a hand-to-mouth existence with half a dozen wayward children, two of whom had already sullied the good name of their father by constant run-ins with the law.

It took a couple of more iftar feasts at Madanpura and Agripada in south Bombay for a friendship to forge. Antulay wanted to tap into Ibrahim Havildar's grass-roots connection with the Muslims in south Bombay.

It didn't take much time for Ibrahim Havildar to unofficially join Antulay's political bandwagon. He even made trips to his assembly constituency, the scenic picture-postcard coastline of Srivardhan, to help boost Antulay's image. He also visited his village, Ambet, in Mhasla taluk.

Antulay was open to ideas that would endear him to the masses. When Ibrahim Havildar drew his attention to the illegal hooch centres in Mumbai and Ratnagiri, and suggested incognito visits to bust them, Antulay lapped up the suggestion.

Antulay and his journalist friend Pramod Navalkar, who was with Bal Thackeray's Shiv Sena, set out on this challenging assignment along with Ibrahim Havildar. The plan was that once Antulay and his friends exited the liquor bars, the secret raiding squads of the police and CID officers would show up to seal the place. Needless to say, the flamboyant Navalkar publicized the tryst in his weekly column in a Marathi paper. The fallout of this was something that Navalkar himself had never anticipated. It was Antulay who walked away with all the kudos.

The media was all praise for Antulay's public relations exercise. In one such frenzied instance, some columnists even referred to him as Napoleon, because of his astute political moves. Antulay earned many more such titles. But it is interesting what finally endeared him to the Muslim community.

In a Muslim public gathering, Ibrahim Havildar once addressed Antulay as '*Iss daur ke Haroon Rashid* (Today's Haroon Rashid).' There are apocryphal stories of Haroon, an Arab ruler of the Abbasid dynasty in 786 AD, who apparently went out among his subjects in disguise during the night to find out how happy they really were. But historians have seriously disputed Haroon's rule as a judicious one and attributed severe violence to him. However, since common perceptions seem to mostly gain precedence over historical facts, the despotic Haroon was hailed as a legendary ruler. This title was lapped up by the Urdu newspapers and Antulay began riding on a new crest of fame and popularity among the Muslim masses.

Fame has a fantastic way of finding fabulous friends and ferreting out formidable foes. Ibrahim Havildar never exploited his budding relationship with Antulay. Despite being summarily dismissed in the Suraiya case, without a fair hearing or an impartial probe, Ibrahim Havildar did not seek Antulay's intervention in the matter.

In the meanwhile, Dawood was done with small-time thuggery. He wanted to join the big league. With little formal education, the boy thought of only one option. Actually, most Muslim boys with little education aspired to be smugglers, having heard of the mythical stories of Haji Mastan. Though Dawood was younger than Sabir, it was he who always came up with the ideas. He was always juggling plans, fielding them before Sabir.

If left to himself, Sabir would have preferred a different world. A world of women and their majestic presence, a world of love, and sex and poetry, of course. Sabir loved poetry, and he was a diehard romantic despite his street-ruffian status. Sabir loved the emotive poetry of Sahir Ludhianvi and romantic songs of Mohammed Rafi.

While Dawood believed in the mafia axiom of '*milee toh maari nahin toh brahmachari* (fuck her if you get lucky, else practise celibacy), Sabir was notorious for being a *khidki-tod aashiq* (staunch romantic)—someone who could spend hours staring out of the window for hours at the girl going about her chores in the opposite building.

At other times, Sabir was spotted at J.J. Square chasing girls passing through the area. Whenever he or his cronies spotted a good-looking girl, they would start following her discreetly. Sabir would stalk her to her house, her coaching classes, to the market and wherever else she went. He would try to woo her and establish contact.

Sabir's other favourite hangout was a tea stall outside the newly established Maharashtra College in Nagpada. The girls who came to college were pretty. He tried to strike up conversations with them by showering them with praises in Urdu. He was fluent in Urdu and could conduct charming conversations. But no sooner did the girls realize that Sabir was a school dropout and a loafer, they shunned him. Sabir would feel heartbroken for a while but then move on to his next conquest in no time.

Dawood had often tried to reason with Sabir, saying, 'We are old enough to find work and change the circumstances of our family. Why should we live in abject poverty and squalor? We need to support our siblings. We need to give our parents a comfortable life.'

Sabir being the elder brother didn't take Dawood seriously for a long time. However, after Dawood attacked Bashu and went on to rob a bank van at Carnac Bunder, Sabir woke up to the realization that Dawood had a propensity to court danger, which could have disastrous consequences for the family.

Dawood had to spend several months in jail for the robbery. It was Ibrahim Havildar who helped the crime branch of the Bombay Police in facilitating his son's arrest. The crime branch had managed to arrest all the accused and had launched an expeditious prosecution. Sabir felt he had let his younger brother down. If only he had not whiled away his time at J.J. Square, he could have probably checked his brother's recklessness. Dawood had been egging him on for so long but he had been careless, and now Dawood was branded a criminal for life. A jail record in a family where the father used to be a part of the police force was something that didn't go down well with Sabir.

Sabir made up his mind to mend his ways. He would be there for Dawood at all times to prevent further misadventures. Despite his yearning for romantic rendezvous with beautiful girls, Sabir agreed to pay attention to Dawood's plans. Dawood always kept Sabir in the loop, according him the respect due to an older brother. When the topic of venturing into the business of smuggling came up, it was Sabir who was told about it first. Dawood always sought his approval. And Sabir listened to Dawood because his brother was sharp and very clever with money matters.

'All the big-league smugglers like Haji Mastan and Yusuf Patel need manpower and daring youths to assist them in landing. We can use our Young Party members for the purpose. Anyway, with hardly any education, the boys of the Young Party are jobless. On the promise of some income, they would readily do our bidding. We can help the big-time smugglers in the transport of silver to Vasai–Virar and land gold and other contraband items whenever the consignment arrives. I am told the landing happens only once a month.'

After green-lighting the idea, Sabir roped in members of the Young Party and joined Dawood's new project. For the first time, a criminal gang had been fashioned out of a sociopolitical group. The outfit eventually became notorious as the 'Dawood–Sabir gang', with Dawood's name preceding Sabir's because Dawood was involved hands-on while Sabir's attention towards the business wavered often. Once entrenched in the gang, the young men landed several consignments. This was called '*maal utarna*'.

The landings of smuggled goods took place at the Cuffe Parade quay, Shivaji Park beach, Versova, Chembur and the Vashi creek.

But for a young man like Dawood the job soon began to pall. The group realized that their earnings were a fraction of what the kingpin was earning. It was Sabir who suggested that they should talk to Ibrahim Havildar's friend Rashid Shaikh who had a lot of connections in the UAE and Kuwait. Rashid's frequent trips to Dubai and his constant meetings with the

Arab sheikhs had earned him the sobriquet of 'Rashid Arba'. Rashid Arba also believed in the liberal use of foul language. Every sentence he spoke had a lot of abuses and expletives, so much so that people were often hesitant to talk to him.

An arrogant man to the core, Arba would never have met Dawood and Sabir, who came from an impoverished background. But the Dongri grapevine was abuzz with the news that Antulay and Ibrahim Havildar were good friends. There was no way that Arba could refuse to meet the boys.

During the several meetings that the brothers had with Arba, he lectured the Kaskar boys that they should learn to capitalize on their father's friendship with Antulay. Both Sabir and Dawood were taken aback. *What friendship?* they thought to themselves. Their father's station in life was a world apart from Antulay's. Besides, they knew their father's limitations. But they kept their thoughts to themselves.

'Bombay coasts and landing corners are now under increased surveillance and constant watch by the police and the customs and DRI sleuths. It is now imperative to look for landing spots beyond Bombay that are safer and less complicated,' Arba cautioned them. 'Antulay's constituency in Srivardhan is a coastal region. You have to simply boast of your father's connections with Antulay, assert your clout and convert those jetties into landing spots,' Arba said very casually.

Since the boys were uninitiated in the art of smuggling, Arba was happy to share more information on the subject. 'The village and district administration in the coastal areas of Konkan can be bought off easily. Which lowly clerk or officer would dare to antagonize a minister from the constituency? Are they going to check with Antulay?' said Arba to reassure them.

In all the time they had known Arba, this was the first time the brothers managed a faint smile.

'*Tumhare saath kaam karke kisi ka kya faayda hoga? Haan, agar tumnein kuch aise landing spots bana liye jo sirf tumhare honge aur uspar sirf tumhara maal utrega, toh tumhari monopoly ho jayegi market mein* (Why would someone want to work with you unless you have some distinct advantage? You need to have a few landing spots of your own which will give you the edge of monopoly in the market).' Arba fired them up.

Before going to Antulay's constituency, Sabir left for his village in Mumke in Ratnagiri district. He began work on capturing the various landing spots that could be exclusively theirs for the unhindered landing of electronics, gold biscuits, watches and other such contraband. Sabir got the influential people of several villages to ensure their tacit support to him. Being the eldest son of Ibrahim Havildar helped; besides, Sabir had a certain charm and persuasive powers, which his other brothers seriously lacked. Sabir's gift of the gab could turn difficult situations in his favour. Sometimes he used the religion card, sometimes their common Konkani heritage and culture. In the end he made sure that the fishermen and other locals were on his side.

After Mumke, Sabir and his boys went to Srivardhan and Mhasla to look for advantageous spots for their landing operations. Most of the jetties in Mhasla and Dighi (in the Raigad district) were easily usurped for their landings. The locals swore to help the Dawood–Sabir gang. The corrupt village administration and even some customs officers agreed to connive with them in the smuggling operations. Those who were not complicit were, of course, under the impression that the brothers were family friends of Antulay's, and thought that if they messed with the boys, they would antagonize the minister.

Sabir and Dawood were so clever about using the combined methods of coercion and corruption to have their way on their favoured landing spots that their rivals in Bombay were left scratching their heads for a long time. They could not figure out how the brothers had managed to acquire the spots so easily. After the first few landings, both brothers were ecstatic about their small triumph. These small successes ensured a few things. Dawood and Sabir became more confident of pulling off such feats consistently as they did not face any resistance from the local police or customs officials, an indication that the government machinery had been greased smoothly. And because the locals managed to make a handsome income through an operation that barely lasted a few hours, they built a long-lasting bond with Dawood and his brothers and were also subservient to them.

Sabir and Dawood never publicly used Antulay's name lest it backfire, but because everybody knew Ibrahim Kaskar was in Antulay's camp, they decided to err on the side of caution. The coastal areas of Konkan are a couple of hours' drive from Mumbai. When Sabir and Dawood fixed their landing spots there, they would never have anticipated how these locations would yield such rich dividends later and turn them into multibillionaires—and, on the flip side, how they would also spell doom for Dawood.

Almost two decades later, in January 1993, when Tiger Memon, the brain behind the Bombay serial blasts of 12 March 1993, wanted to bring in a huge quantity of RDX and weapons from Pakistan, he knew that Dawood–Sabir's landing spots would be the safest and also that he would need Dawood's blessings to ensure that the villagers allowed the consignment to land in Raigad. The massive amount of contraband could only be smuggled into the city through the

Raigad coasts. The locals ended up paying a heavy price for their loyalty to Dawood, along with several customs and police officials, who were later arrested and prosecuted.

But way back in the late 1970s, it was inconceivable that these landing spots would be used for import of terror in the country. Dawood wanted to use it only for expanding and increasing his smuggling activities. He was only looking to increase his turnover by bringing in multiple consignments of gold and other contraband to augment his profits.

Financing a consignment before it is shipped from Dubai or Singapore is a major hurdle for any smuggler in the city. Not many people would be willing to risk their funds for a consignment whose fate was hanging in the balance. In the case of established players like Haji Mastan, Yusuf Patel or Bashu Dada, they knew they could hedge their investment but Dawood was a late entrant and was yet to find his footing.

Every motor launch that left the Dubai coasts carried goods worth over at least Rs 25–40 lakh. In those days it was a staggering amount, and it was not possible for one investor to singularly finance a transaction. So every consignment was jointly funded by numerous businessmen in the city. Rashid Arba was one such investor, but for some reason the Kaskar brothers did not like him. They were exploring options for other sponsors.

It was at this juncture that Sabir came to the rescue, proving to be far more resourceful than Dawood ever expected. Sabir had the ability to always be enterprising and connect the dots. He had made inroads into the Marwari and Gujarati community while selling silver and gold to them. Some seths at the Kalbadevi bullion market were eating out of Sabir's hands. They were doing business with Sabir more out of the love for lucre than the fear of his ruffian ways. In his inimitable style,

Sabir had also managed romps with a couple of rich Marwari women. The alliances were short-lived though.

His strongest business association was forged with Kamal Chadha of Colaba and his brother-in-law Mahendra Choradia, who had a huge sea-facing mansion in Worli. Chadha and Choradia were engaged in money laundering and other allied businesses. They gladly agreed to be venture capitalists for Dawood in an era where seed money was the lifeblood of smuggling. Years later, when Dawood was locked in an internecine gang war with his rivals, Choradia was brutally hacked to death by the Arun Gawli gang, as they knew his importance in the rise of Dawood's criminal empire.

With help from Choradia and his hawala set-up, Dawood had begun making a neat profit in the smuggling business. Sabir's connections had immensely bolstered Dawood's enterprise. The only lacunae in the whole plan was that it was lopsided. While he had stitched up all the loose ends at the Bombay side, he was totally at sea about the Dubai part. He wished he could bag a big deal directly from Dubai.

Dawood needed a strong connection in Dubai. While the brothers were racking their brains, thinking every permutation and combination, Sabir came up with a lead: '*Khalid Bhai ko bhul gaye* (We forgot about Khalid Bhai).'

It came to him in a flash. Dawood recalled that it was Khalid who had gone to Dubai and not only established a successful passage for silver from India but also convinced Bashu to get into gold smuggling. And how could he forget that Khalid was the first smuggler to deal in precious stones, which he got from Dubai.

Dawood was convinced that Khalid was the man of the hour. His Dubai contacts were priceless. Khalid could help him with the Dubai end, which had been a blind spot for Dawood so far. He could learn a lot from Khalid.

If he had to reign supreme in the smuggling business, then he had to convince Khalid to join forces with him.

17

Dawood's Overtures

Every time the character played by Randhir Kapoor gulps down his drink, Vijayendra Ghatge is quick to refill the glass with more liquor. The villain in Ghatge wants Kapoor to get drunk beyond his senses. Actually, the drinking binge is a prelude to a macabre murder plot. Ghatge wants to bump off Kapoor after getting him sozzled to the gills. Soon two toughies walk in and join the table where Kapoor is getting drunk. One of the two toughies is Khalid.

Khalid enters the bar dressed in a dark-blue jacket and light denim, while his crony is wearing a grey jacket and trousers. They pull out chairs to join Ghatge and Kapoor in their drinking spree. After a while, Ghatge lifts his head and gives a little nod. Khalid wastes no time in understanding the unspoken signal. They are Ghatge's henchmen and are here to kill Kapoor. They drive him to a deserted spot and violently assault him with the intention of killing him. Kapoor, totally inebriated, fails to put up a fight against the three goons.

No, this is not a skirmish straight out of a mafia plot involving Khalid. It is a scene from a Bollywood blockbuster called *Kasme Vaade*, which released in April 1978. The movie boasted an A-list star cast that included Amitabh Bachchan, Amjad Khan, Rakhi, Neetu Singh and Randhir Kapoor.

In the second half of the 1970s, Amitabh Bachchan had emerged as a phenomenon. Every movie he starred in was a huge hit. The Hindi-film industry had suddenly discovered its Gregory Peck. Such was his aura and charisma that female actors were vying to be cast opposite him, villains were willing to get killed so that they could share screen space with the great Bachchan himself and even the most arrogant actors did not mind playing second lead to him.

It was the elaborate set of a luxury bar, replete with ornate chandeliers and rich mahogany tables. Ghatge had lured Kapoor here to impress him with the ambience and the fawning butlers serving vintage wine.

Khalid is seen mumbling some inaudible pleasantries as he shakes hands with Ghatge. The scene, which was followed by a hurried fight sequence, folded up in a jiffy. Khalid was sorely disappointed with his teeny-weeny role in the movie, and to top it all he was not even paid a single dime. The only consolation was that he had acted in an Amitabh Bachchan movie.

Two years ago, Bachchan walked down memory lane as he celebrated thirty-eight years of *Kasme Vaade* by posting several pictures and articles on social media. He observed that it was the most popular Indian movie in Israel.

Khalid's Hindi movie sojourn happened purely because of his wrestling past. It was a chance offer where he was set to appear alongside Dara Singh in a Jeetendra and Leena Chandavarkar action thriller called *Nalayak*. Dara Singh had a supporting role in the movie in which he helped Jeetendra fight off some thugs. At the time Jeetendra had yet to establish himself as an action hero and the directors had decided to use Dara Singh to help him out in the role.

Khalid was asked to play a man Friday to Dara Singh. In this movie too Khalid had a peripheral role, but Dara Singh could be heard calling out a couple of times to 'Ganpat', Khalid's character. Khalid had signed up for *Nalayak* before *Kasme Vaade* but the former's release got pushed by several months and *Kasme Vaade* ended up hitting the theatres earlier.

The Mumbai mafia had always been obsessed with Bollywood and all its glamour. Haji Mastan, Karim Lala and every other don in Bombay at the time wanted to be associated with Hindi cinema. It earned them respectability, and the bonus was that they could be photographed with the reigning stars of the era, including Dilip Kumar. In fact, Mastan even produced several Muslim-centric social movies to shed his image of a smuggler and turn over a new leaf as a film producer.

When word got around that Khalid was working as a goon in the movies, some mafia members mocked him while others interpreted it as his infatuation with Bollywood. Dawood, who had seen the real heroics of Khalid and knew his actual stature and calibre, could not tolerate such frivolous discussions. Dawood reckoned that Khalid was going through a rough patch after his separation from Bashu, which may be why he had agreed to act in cameo roles in Hindi films.

Dawood had always thought that Khalid had wasted himself at the Social Club. Dawood wanted to work with his mentor as he understood Khalid's felicity and fearlessness, an unbeatable lethal combination in the underworld. Khalid's special skills and unconventional thinking had made Bashu richer and stronger. Had they continued to be a team, they could have surpassed all their competitors and rivals to emerge as the most powerful gang in the city. Dawood was aware that he would not be anywhere in the reckoning if Bashu Dada and Khalid had remained steadfast as a team.

But Bashu's jealousy and lack of foresight had proved to be the gang's undoing. Dawood decided to meet Khalid to persuade him to return to smuggling.

It had been over five years since Khalid had walked out of Teli Mohalla, out of Bashu Dada's life and then abandoned the business altogether. Khalid had been waiting for some opportunity to come his way that would propel him to a financially lucrative venture. However, nothing worthwhile had been proposed to him. Years had passed and he had now started feeling ennui and stagnation.

He had made incessant efforts to find peace in many ways. In fact, he even went to his home town of Harda after a long hiatus and donated a lot of money as charity to various masjids and madrasas. The idea behind philanthropy is that it cannot be a one-off gesture. Charity needs to be a continuous effort. It has to have meaning and purpose. After donating lakhs of rupees towards various charitable causes and mosques, Khalid felt good for a while. But soon he felt the same emptiness gnawing inside him—the feeling that he could generate loads of money, if only he had some backing.

His aspirations to share screen space with Amitabh Bachchan had also come to naught. Though he had a fleeting background appearance in *Nalayak* with Jeetendra and Dara Singh, in *Kasme Vaade,* Bachchan was miles away from the frame. Khalid's dreams of working with Bachchan were shattered. Business-wise Khalid, too, was not very happy as his financial resources were dwindling. He did not have the required wherewithal and the gang network set-up needed to run a smuggling syndicate independently, else he would have launched his own enterprise long ago. He missed his smuggling days. He missed the excitement, the power and the cat-and-mouse game with the law-enforcement agencies, but mostly he missed the money.

It was one of those soul-searching moments that occurred when Khalid was at the club, when Dawood dropped by and took him out for dinner. During the meal, Dawood gave Khalid a detailed low-down of his smuggling exploits.

Dawood told him about how he and Sabir had monopolized the landing spots of Raigad, Dighi and other spots on the Konkan and Srivardhan coasts. 'We rule the roost there. No outsider can ever use those landing spots,' Dawood had said with a certain sense of braggadocio.

He also told Khalid about how he had developed close business relations with the top bullion and gold traders in Kalbadevi. He name-dropped several reputed Marwari and Gujarati seths from Bombay and Surat. Khalid's heart raced at the information. He told him that they had sounded out some Pakistani smugglers in Dubai who had agreed to do business with them in Bombay. Dawood was sharing with Khalid his intricate and exclusively cultivated business blueprint, without keeping any secrets or withholding any names or contacts. Khalid felt a sudden rush of affection, delight and admiration at his protégé's financial success and rapid strides in the smuggling business. Dawood had done very well for himself and the best part was that he was quite open and candid about his business activities, and was confiding in him without any insecurities or fears that people in such businesses usually display.

When Dawood was done talking, he abruptly made an offer, without any preamble, to Khalid, saying, '*Bhai, aa jao, mujh se haath milalo. Milkar dhanda karte hain,* (Brother, join hands with me, let's do business together).' Khalid knew that Dawood did not have the eloquence and was usually brutally direct to the extent of being hurtfully blunt. But this was just too much for him to absorb. Khalid was totally taken aback and pleasantly surprised to hear of the offer from Dawood. Khalid could never have expected that someone who had such a well-established business and who had smoothened all the kinks in the process with the best available resources could even think of inviting an outsider as a partner, to share the spoils.

At the time, Dawood's gang was not known as the D-Gang but was referred to as the Dawood–Sabir gang. Despite being the older sibling, Sabir received second billing in the gang and Dawood had the upper hand. Khalid had a good equation with Dawood but he was not so sure about Sabir. 'Why don't you check with Sabir if he is okay with me coming in?'

Dawood's reply was a shocker, '*Agar mujhe do mein se kisi ek ki baat manni padi, toh main hamesha aap ki baat manoonga, aur bhai ko mana loonga* (If I have to choose between Sabir and you, then I will always give preference to you and convince Sabir to follow suit).' Khalid was totally floored at this humility and affection shown by Dawood. There was no reason for him to hesitate.

Khalid immediately gave his consent and Dawood smiled. Khalid rose from the table and gave a bear hug to a much shorter and thinner Dawood, almost lifting him off his feet. It was a genuine and sincere embrace that only a Pathan could give with all his intensity and fervour.

Perhaps Khalid interpreted the whole situation in a positive sense. He presumed that Dawood, who had been a fan and well-wisher so far, now wanted to take the relationship to the next level and work as business partners. Khalid, in all his naivety, attributed this offer of a business alliance to Dawood's innate nobility and strength of character.

But Khalid did not know that his protégé, Dawood, had slowly become a hardcore businessman, with a focus only on multiplying his profits. He was not a hapless teenager any more. The boy had now developed fangs and was ready to claw his way to the top of the pile. At this juncture, Dawood was clearly looking for friends with benefits, a concept that Bombay's socialites figured out only much later—Dawood had already perfected this idea in the 1970s. He had done his calculations clearly and realized that Khalid's association would only enhance his profits. Khalid had amazing contacts in Dubai and knew the logistics of the business so well that he would monitor the gold's movement from coast to coast, making Dawood a millionaire in no time.

Another factor that worked for Dawood was the timing. Lady Luck seemed to always be on his side. It was the era of the Emergency and most smugglers were behind bars. Haji Mastan, Yusuf Patel and several others had been incarcerated by Indira Gandhi. Dawood, who had always secretly nursed a desire to overtake Mastan's legendary reign, decided that this was the most opportune time to accelerate his efforts and make inroads into Mastan's close-knit group of buyers and business associates.

Mastan had managed to reach the top only because he had Arab patrons who staked their money on gold smuggling for him. Other smugglers worked with Pakistani syndicates who always preferred Karachi buyers. Khalid was the only man who had developed solid bonds with the Arabs, his connections with the Galadari brothers being well known. Dawood knew that the Galadaris trusted Khalid and that this friendship could be exploited to further his business interests.

Dawood needed Khalid to persuade the Galadaris to become their main partner in Dubai.

18

The Five-Man Army

Even before the muezzin climbed atop the minaret of a famous British-era masjid in south Bombay, the faithful were already walking towards the mosque in anticipation of the azan, the mandatory call for prayer of the namaz-e-asr. Muslims from the neighbouring shops, hotels, offices and residences began converging.

Suddenly, a white Fiat drew up outside the masjid. Two out of the five men who emerged were in their twenties while the other three were in their early thirties. All five tied a handkerchief to cover their heads as they walked resolutely towards the Hujra Mohalla Masjid.

The old-timers of the area and the skullcap- and handkerchief-wearing worshippers were taken aback when they saw the occupants of the car. These were no men of God. Their notoriety preceded them. They were the black sheep of the area. Men who lived by the sword and who dared anybody to question them.

The men, of course, were not oblivious to the effect they had on the bystanders. Some of them who knew these men in passing threw them a hurried salaam before slipping away to another corner of the masjid, away from them. Once inside the masjid, they went to the wet wudu area in the large prayer hall for the pre-namaz ablutions. And then they prayed together, much to the astonishment of the onlookers, who had presumed the men had walked in to settle scores with someone. After finishing their prayers, the group retreated to a corner of the mosque with a copy of the Holy Quran in their hands. In a solemn and spiritual gesture, all of them placed their hands on the cover of the Quran, as if taking an oath. 'We will watch out for each other and never betray each other,' they declared solemnly in unison.

These five men were among the city's most notorious gangsters. Dawood Ibrahim, Sabir Ibrahim, Khalid Pehelwan and two other toughies known as Anjum Sayed and Lal Khan Pathan.

They had just watched the 1969 Hollywood cult classic *The Five-Man Army*. It was the story of five reluctant heroes helping the Mexican Revolution by robbing a gold consignment from a train. For Dawood and his team the takeaway was 'United we stand, divided we fall,' hence the little detour to the masjid for some good old-fashioned spiritual affirmation. The ringside viewers outside the mosque, who were initially taken aback at this newfound love for God, had no idea that these five were actually taking an oath to be more violent and greedy in their pursuit of supremacy among the Bombay mafia.

The Dawood–Sabir gang had crystallized its plans to set up the most powerful smuggling syndicate in the city. It was Khalid's idea to form a new group, a syndicate that gave birth to the idea of a five-man army. Khalid had told them that, henceforth, smuggling would be properly regulated and the whole process, right from the procurement, acquisition, supply and distribution of smuggled contraband would be handled the way respected blue-chip companies functioned.

This was a major step towards the corporatization of smuggling. The plan was to involve other ganglords in the area and make them a part of the syndicate. Most of the gold financers and smugglers signed up and promised to be loyal and committed to it, much like the functioning of the bushido, the code of conduct of the Japanese samurai warriors.

The proposition was simple: anyone could invest money in smuggling; they would be entitled to keep 50 per cent of the profits while also contributing 50 per cent to the coffers of the syndicate. The exchequer would finance the smoothening of the logistics—in other words, grease the palms of the law-enforcement agencies like the police and the customs department. The investors were happy that they were not personally exposed in any way to the law and happily contributed their profits to the syndicate because the returns were so high. Times were tough for them, with Indira Gandhi cracking down on black marketeers by imposing the Emergency. They were afraid of midnight raids on their black money and were happy to give it away to the Dawood–Sabir gang to invest it for them.

Between 1975 and 1977, the Bombay mafia was in a tumult. The big fish—Haji Mastan, Karim Lala and Yusuf Patel—were all biding their time in the Arthur Road Jail along with a lot of prominent political personalities. But Bombay was no exception, jails all over India were overflowing with both mafia members and political detenues and other dissenters. But among the middle class in Bombay, there was a huge sense of relief about the arrest of the black marketeers, shady businessmen and ganglords.

People were being charged either under the Maintenance of Internal Security Act (MISA) or the National Security Act (NSA). MISA was a newly promulgated national law in 1971, and was fortified in 1974, which gave sweeping powers to the government and no reprieve to the detenue. Under the law, any accused could be detained without the framing of formal charges against them and be thrown into jail without stringent procedures that are normally followed under the IPC.

The smugglers and the Bombay mafia were quaking in their shoes when Indira Gandhi announced in Parliament her plans to confiscate smugglers' properties. This had never happened before. The Bombay mafia, which had enjoyed a free run and an unhindered growth graph, suddenly seemed to have struck a fatal iceberg. They could not figure out what hit them.

While the big fish were caught early on, the smaller ones also got entangled, but at a later stage. For a while, Dawood Ibrahim, Varadarajan Mudaliar and Arun Gawli also became trapped under the NSA.

A report prepared by the then Bombay police commissioner, S.V. Tankiwala, submitted to the Ministry of Home Affairs claimed, 'As many as 288 smugglers including Haji Mastan and Yusuf Patel were detained and the property of over 177 smugglers were attached.'

Mastan and his cronies tried hiring the most expensive legal luminaries like Ram Jethmalani but Indira Gandhi was relentless. The government also slapped the COFEPOSA Act on Mastan and his ilk. When Mastan and Patel walked out as free men, the battering they had received from the government had done them a world of good! They gave up smuggling and lived a reformed life.

Even if they had intended to pursue smuggling, they found that in twenty-one months their businesses were in a shambles.

Everybody had to start from scratch, as even the local moneybags were now wary. The Emergency had discouraged a lot of reckless businessmen from dubious deals.

Dawood knew that the time was ripe for him to establish his mafia empire, especially on a level playing field. His competition was almost non-existent. The new government, under a new dispensation, was trying to woo the masses.

Gold smuggling was flourishing during the term of the then prime minister Morarji Desai. The post-Emergency era, especially the year 1978, was regarded as a flourishing time for criminals. Dawood was the first to capitalize on this wave.

His reunion with Khalid augured well for him. He knew that Khalid was a potential gold mine, and shook his head and smiled every time he thought of how Bashu Dada could be so stupid as to not recognize and play on Khalid's strengths.

Khalid had never felt as much at home as he did with Dawood. The boy was young, full of life and very bright. He was also fearless and thought much ahead of his times. He made Khalid think on his feet and brought out the best in him. With Bashu, Khalid never knew where he stood in the equation despite having given so much to the gang. But with Dawood he felt like an insider. Dawood made him feel special. There was no insecurity like there was with Bashu. Khalid knew that his association with Dawood would take smuggling to new heights in Bombay.

Khalid immediately made a trip to Dubai and touched base with his brotherlike business partner Abdul Wahab Galadari, who was equally excited to meet Khalid after such a long hiatus.

A lot had happened in Galadari's life too. He had just split from his brothers and had gone on to establish his own empire, which was in direct competition with that of his estranged siblings.

He started a newspaper, *Gulf News*, to compete with his brothers' *Khaleej Times*. If his brothers had their Intercontinental Hotels, he had Hyatt Regency. Rahim and Latif owned the Dubai Bank, Wahab established the Union Bank of the Middle East. He also began investing in London and Singapore, becoming the third-largest Arab investor in Singapore. Wahab wanted to expand his business further in Southeast Asian countries.

Despite his raging ambitions, Wahab could not own businesses in India or invest in any financial enterprise in the country. In fact, the gold king and dollar billionaire, with worldwide clout and influence, had endured a run-in with the Indian government, who had blacklisted his brothers and him for more than a decade.

After the Emergency was recalled in March 1977, the three Galadaris were declared proclaimed offenders by the Indian government on 3 August 1977 under Section 83 of the Code of Criminal Procedure, which deals with the attachment of the properties of fugitives.

The Galadaris' ancestral wealth included apartments and various other properties in Colaba and Cuffe Parade. The youngest brother, Latif, had also attended schools in Bombay. Wahab loved the city and was very fond of India. It was the city and country that had given him his wealth. He knew her seas and her coasts.

As far back as the early 1960s, Wahab had established a smooth smuggling link between Dubai and Bombay and had frequently begun visiting the city through motorboats and dhows along with huge consignments of smuggled gold. In fact, the DRI had no clue of the involvement of a Dubai sheikh in such brazen gold-smuggling expeditions on the Bombay coastline until 1964.

When the DRI sleuths intercepted a dhow off the Ratnagiri coast carrying over 120 kg gold worth over Rs 10 lakh, they discovered that it belonged to Wahab, who was already in Bombay to receive the consignment. The DRI officers immediately arrested Wahab along with twenty-three others, including three customs officers, but Wahab managed to jump bail, sneaked out of Bombay and escaped to Dubai. Wahab was barely twenty-four years old then.

Once on Wahab's trail, the DRI began diligently chasing the Galadari brothers. Wahab was accused in several smuggling cases, including for landing gold at Mafatlal Park in Cuffe Parade in south Bombay and on the Murud coast near Alibag. All these consignments ranged from 120 to over 200 kg, in gold biscuits, and were due to be received at various landing spots along the Ratnagiri coastline. In one case in 1968, Wahab and thirty-eight others were indicted by a customs officer called J.S. Wagh for smuggling over 1000 kg of gold through the Kashid coast in Alibag.

The Indian government had piled up cases against all the Galadaris and men from the syndicate under the simple premise of respondeat superior (which in Latin means 'let the master answer'). As per the doctrine, Abdul would be held responsible for all the smuggling cases even if his brothers or other syndicate members were involved in it. These and other such cases against the Galadari brothers had rendered them persona non grata in India, while they had totally clean records everywhere else in the world. No country or agencies had dared or bothered to declare them wanted, it is not exactly known whether this was because of their influence or affluence.

India Today had reported, 'All the brothers had been proclaimed offenders in India in 1977 after the government failed to bring them to trial on charges of smuggling gold into India while smuggling silver out of the country.'

The DRI wanted the Galadari brothers to be prosecuted in a trial court and hence the 1977 proclamation order was a big feather in their cap. The agency was aware that it would not be possible to extradite them from Dubai given their clout and connections, but at least the Galadaris would not be able to flit in and out of the country at whim.

Wahab was dismayed by the court's proclamation order against him and his brothers. He was thrilled to see Khalid at a time when he was contemplating his next course of action in India. Khalid told him he wanted to pick up from where he had left off five years ago, and Wahab welcomed Khalid's decision. He was, after all, the most influential gold dealer in the UAE despite an existing cabal of Pakistani smugglers in the region.

During the conversation, Wahab realized that Khalid had become much wiser and pragmatic and in a position to take decisions all by himself without the sword of Damocles in the form of Bashu looming over his head.

The deal they struck was simple and lucrative for all the parties concerned. Wahab would give them gold consignments on the Dubai coast and Khalid would have to organize the launch and its safe passage to Bombay's shores. Once they transported the gold to Indian markets, it would be the responsibility of the Dawood–Sabir gang to distribute and sell the gold. Wahab instantly liked the proposal and shook hands with Khalid, green-lighting the agreement.

With Wahab's support, Khalid and Dawood began their second innings in gold smuggling in Bombay. Right from the word go, the venture was a huge success. The duo's hunger and hunger for profits and power kept them on their toes and facilitated the continuous rolling of gold and silver landings into their turf.

With this megacorporation of smugglers in place, Khalid now focused his attention on the fortification of the Dawood gang. He realized that the Dawood–Sabir gang only had Muslims and no Hindus.

Khalid's childhood in Madhya Pradesh and the friendships he had forged during his college and wrestling days with Hindus had given him a progressive and secular outlook in life. His interactions with Hindus made him stand apart from other Muslims who tended to be insular. It was an absolutely new and unheard-of philosophy in the Bombay mafia. A Muslim Pathan asking his fellow Muslim brethren to include Hindu men in the gang to make the gang stronger and lend it character. Dawood, who never differed with Khalid, immediately agreed to his suggestion.

To walk the talk, Khalid began hiring Hindu boys in the gang. Initially, he got in touch with some of his Hindu friends in Bhopal and Harda and recruited them. The lure of lucre and Khalid's charisma was the main draw. Khalid's friends began trooping into Bombay. Subsequently, Khalid also recruited local Maharashtrian boys into the gang. With the admission of Hindu men in the conglomerate, which included Rama Naik, Babu Reshim, Philips Pandhare, Ashok Joshi, Satish Raje and others, the Dawood gang became formidable. The gang structure was now secular and had become a major force to reckon with in the city. The city's moneybags like Rashid Arba and other members of the syndicate were satisfied as everyone was making a decent profit. But not all people can be kept happy all the time. The Pathans, who included Karim Lala, Rahim Lala, Samad Khan, Amirzada and Alamzeb, were quite resentful of Dawood's success and growth.

For them the biggest fly in the ointment was Khalid, a Pathan to boot, one of their own, who stood like an indestructible wall, shielding Dawood from them.

They knew that if they wanted to ambush Dawood, they would have to demolish the wall first.

19

An Undercover Wedding

A wedding function without the groom in attendance can upset the calmest fathers-in-law-to-be. The bride's family was visibly nervous, and this particular father was doubly anxious because the groom had suddenly requested a change in venue. The shamiana on the terrace had all the required decorations for a wedding—twinkling fairly lights in different colours, streamers and lots of tube-lights to brighten the place. The aluminium folding chairs were neatly arranged and the *dastarkhwan* (an ornate spread on which food is served in Muslim gatherings) was a long row of slender tables arranged vertically with a plastic sheet on top.

Generally, Pathan weddings are a riot of colour and cacophony. As the community itself is known for its boisterous and loud nature, their weddings are their showcase. Men do the Pashto Attan dance in beautiful synchronicity, dressed in Pathani suits with a waistcoat. The groom arrives in a well-decorated car, and there is lots of rich food on the menu.

That evening, most of the bride and groom's family was bedecked in traditional costumes. The men were attired in

Pathani suits, a long kameez and a salwar, with shoes. Some of them had on round Afghani caps. But there was no revelry and no cackle of laughter—even among the women at the segregated wedding venue. The only compensation for sore eyes was the sight of the ladies glittering in their best.

The bride's father, Sayed Lakhte Pacha, seemed to be visibly anxious and tense. The nikah was supposed to be solemnized immediately after the Isha prayer, which is the fifth and last prayer of the day and is wound up usually around 8.30 p.m. It was an interminable wait for the man as the groom was nowhere in sight.

Both the qazis, who separately represented the bride and groom, had arrived and been told that the groom was on his way. The clock was ticking and the guests were getting restless. Pacha was conscious of the muffled whispers discussing his daughter Husn Bano's missing groom. He had never expected that the auspicious occasion of his daughter's wedding would be such a psychological ordeal for him.

Pacha still remembers vividly the day Dawood's father, Ibrahim Havildar, and community elder Sayed Abbas Pacha, had come to him and sought his daughter's hand for Khalid Khan. Both Ibrahim Havildar and Sayed Sahib had a considerable stature among the Pathans. When they vouched for Khalid's integrity and unblemished credentials and pedigree, Lakhte Pacha could not refuse their proposal. The Pathans, being an ethnic tribe, generally prefer alliances within their own community. Khalid seemed to be the right match for his daughter. Lakhte Pacha wasted no time in giving his consent to Ibrahim Havildar and Sayed Sahib.

The dates were finalized and the marriage was supposed to materialize within a few weeks. However, without warning, mere days before the wedding, the venue was changed and the preparations were carried out under much secrecy. Like most Indians, the girl's family hardly have a say in such matters. Lakhte Pacha was not completely happy, but he reluctantly agreed to a low-key celebration. Right from the number of guests, who were just a handful in number, every aspect of the marriage was organized on a conservative scale.

A couple of buses were hired and the whole baraat had quietly departed from Mumbai to a secret location in Mumbra, which is over 40 km away from Mumbai. Mumbra is considered India's largest Muslim ghetto. At the time, of course, Mumbra was not as chaotic, disorderly or densely populated as it is today. But the idea behind having a wedding in Mumbra, which even then had a sizeable Muslim population, was to deflect attention away from the groom.

A colourful shamiana had been erected on the terrace of Rahmaniya building, situated close to the Mumbra railway station. The fully curved station was, at the time, over 115 years old, built by the British soon after the construction of the Victoria Terminus in 1853.

The history of Mumbra city is much older and has had traces of the Mughal imprint for over 400 years. However, it was renamed after the Mumbadevi Temple around 150 years ago. Earlier it was called Umra by the Mughal army, which used the Reti Bandar port as a shipbuilding yard, and the township was the entry point towards Durgadi Fort in Kalyan, known as Callian in those days.

After the communal riots in 1984, Mumbra became a hub for all Muslims from Mumbai and elsewhere who converged here because they thought it was safe and also because of the dirt-cheap real-estate prices and the easy availability of cubbyhole-sized houses.

Today, Mumbra is teeming with over 20 lakh residents, of whom over 90 per cent are Muslims. For students of social sciences, Mumbra is a classic example of Muslim ghettoization in India, which occurred much before the 2002 Gujarat riots.

At the time of his marriage to Husn Bano in 1980, Khalid was thirty years old. Most men in his community got married by the age of twenty-five, but Khalid had been busy establishing his career and there was nobody who took interest in getting him married. So, after his proposal for marriage was accepted, he was euphoric. But he was not able to revel in this feeling as fate threw a spanner in the works. Just a week before the wedding, Dawood gave him a shocker: '*Khalid Bhai, Chandi pakdi gayi hai and usmein aap ko wanted dikhaya hai* (Your silver consignment has been confiscated by customs and your name is now on their wanted list).' Khalid was stunned by this nugget of information.

In his decade-long career in the Bombay mafia, Khalid had managed to smuggle massive amounts of gold, silver and diamonds and other contraband without ever being under the scanner of the customs or the police. He had managed to be discreet and careful so there was no dossier on him.

And, eventually, lo and behold, his name cropped up after his consignment, comprising thirty measly silver bricks, was confiscated by the DRI! The DRI, along with Mumbai Police, had declared him wanted. While other mafia members wear the 'most wanted' tag as an accolade and even feel that it boosts their value on the virtual mafia stock exchange, Khalid always believed in operating below the radar. He believed that one only got freedom and flexibility to operate in the smuggling business if they remained obscure and anonymous. This credo had helped him remain safe during the Emergency, when big mafia dons and their cronies were cooling their heels in various jails.

When the government turned on the heat, he knew it was time to switch careers. He dabbled as a character artist in Hindi movies to tide over the Emergency era.

That evening, when Dawood dropped the bombshell, Khalid was pensive. Having the law-enforcement agencies on your heels, in hot pursuit, when you are embarking on a new personal journey was very unsettling. It would also be a setback to his myriad business activities. He could no longer fly frequently to Dubai on his business trips. It would also affect his marriage plans. It was then decided that the venue of the wedding be changed. While the Mumbai Police and customs officers would be hunting for him within the jurisdiction of Bombay city limits, they would not be able to imagine in their wildest dreams that he would be married in Mumbra, which was beyond their jurisdiction.

Thus, the nikah and reception were kept closely guarded secrets. People did not know even the name of the groom until they saw Khalid, followed by Dawood, climbing the terrace of the Rahmaniya building. Both men had decided not to travel by road and had instead opted for a local suburban train to Mumbra. The crowd would provide them good cover as they would be able to slink out of the city and make it to the wedding.

Once they reached the venue, a series of rituals—including the *sehra* (headdress worn by the groom), the stipulation of mahr (alimony for the bride), *salam karai* (where the groom bows and salaams to everyone)—were performed with relative ease and focus. The whole function went off uneventfully. Dawood was personally delighted as his father, Ibrahim, had played a pivotal role in the marriage and contributed tremendously to the safe passage and organization of the ceremony.

Over the past few months, Dawood and Khalid had forged a stronger bond, closer than brothers and as thick as thieves. Khalid was Dawood's childhood idol and hero. For Khalid, Dawood was a confidante and a friend. Since the time they had teamed up in 1978, they had weathered many a storm and surmounted several catastrophes.

The Pathans of Mumbai had never approved of Dawood having the upper hand, whether with regard to gangland equations or smuggling. Amirzada and Alamzeb were two bloodthirsty cousins from the Pathan syndicate who had no qualms about killing anyone. They aspired to topple Dawood and gain supremacy in the underworld.

Any friend of Dawood's was their arch-enemy and a marked man. Iqbal Natiq was the editor of the Urdu tabloid *Raazdaar* (The Confidant). It was published from Dongri, and Natiq, who was essentially a crime reporter, was an idealist and quite fearless. Coming from a world inhabited by dishonesty, venality, distrust, violence and treachery, Dawood found Natiq to be the antithesis of all that he had known. Natiq embodied goodness, and Dawood was surprisingly very fond of him. Dawood would often rib him, 'You can't change the world with a rag of a paper. If you want change, become an elected representative.'

Dawood convinced Natiq to contest the Lok Sabha elections in 1977 from Umarkhadi. Natiq lost, of course, but there was no twinge of regret. He was completely content bringing out his little tabloid that was filled with sensational stories that even mainstream publications did not boast of. One such story became his death warrant.

Amirzada and Alamzeb used to hide their smuggled goods at the Chawla Guest House on Ibrahim Rahimtullah Road. Saeed Batla and Ayub Lala, both hooligans, ran errands for them and did their bidding. When a newly-wed couple checked into the guest house, the two men raped the bride and killed the groom. The murder remained unsolved and the police had no clue until Natiq exposed them on the front page of his newspaper. Soon other newspapers followed suit and the cops were forced to arrest Saeed and Ayub. The arrests and negative exposure seriously undermined the clout of the Pathans in the area.

After their release on bail, Saeed Batla and Ayub Lala plotted their revenge. One night, they forced Natiq to leave his house and accompany them to a lonely place. Natiq was tortured all night, stabbed multiple times by Saeed and Ayub and then dumped at the Mahim Creek. Before he died, Natiq told the police about his torture. 'Saeed kept stabbing me and kept repeating, "*Dawood ke kutte, bula usko tujhe bachane* (Dawood's dog, now dare to call him to save you)."'

Natiq succumbed to his injuries, leaving Dawood totally devastated and crushed. Dawood had never known bereavement earlier, that too of such a close friend and ally. Dawood was mourning Natiq and spending his days and weeks in melancholy until Khalid promised to hunt for Natiq's killers.

Dawood's grief was alleviated after Khalid chopped off Saeed's limbs and inflicted death on Ayub. But what he did not bargain for was the intense animosity of Alamzeb and Amirzada. They knew that Dawood would be their nemesis if they didn't catch him first. For the first time in their lives, the Pathans, who generally weren't scared of anybody, felt a quiver of fear when they thought of Dawood and his rapid rise in the mafia rungs. They hated his guts and they hated his mad mind. He was always a step ahead of them. They had a syndicate, while he was just a newbie, but he had found a way of doing all the right things and getting all the right people on his side. The duo decided that they needed all the Pathans to unite to fight Dawood. They succeeded in rallying the Pathans for their cause, but Khalid was the only Pathan who was steadfastly loyal, resisted the pressure of the Pathan syndicate and refused to leave Dawood.

The Alamzeb–Amirzada duo carried out several attacks on Dawood and Khalid. They survived by a whisker in some cases, while in other situations they fended off their attackers with the help of their quick reflexes. Even when Dawood and Sabir were bound for hajj and had donned their *ihrams* (white pilgrim robe) while on their way to the holy city of Mecca, Alamzeb and Amirzada were close on their heels at the Haj House.

As they searched for the brothers at Haj House, they learnt that Dawood and Sabir had already left for the airport in a bus ferrying the hajis. The Pathans were hell-bent on killing Dawood outside the airport, even if he was in the white robe, which was considered sacred. They raced their bike like madmen in an attempt to overtake the bus and intercept it before it reached the airport. They wanted to make mincemeat of both Dawood and Sabir, at a time when they were disarmed and had no bodyguards to defend them. But those were the days when cars were few and far between and the bus managed to reach the airport before Alamzeb and Amirzada caught up with them. It was destiny that Dawood had already crossed the security gate of Santa Cruz Airport and was safely ensconced inside it, beyond the reach of death. Those were the days when this airport was also used for international air travel as Sahar International Airport came up only in 1981. Expectedly, Khalid had gone to see Dawood off. As he came out of the visitor's gallery at Santa Cruz, he spotted the Pathans with their men and weapons. Khalid knew that that they had come with dangerous intentions. He immediately braced for a fight as he always carried a weapon.

The Pathans too had seen Khalid and realized that he was spoiling for a fight now. They knew that it was the wrong place and time to engage in a skirmish while their main target Dawood was not even present. They deferred the battle for a later date and abruptly left the scene in a haste. Khalid was disappointed about letting them escape, but in his book a true warrior never chased the deserters.

This aborted attempt on Dawood's life became a hot topic among the mafia. Some said Dawood was fortunate while others said that he was blessed with a cat's proverbial nine lives. They also alluded to Khalid's courage and willingness to take the Pathans on single-handedly at the airport.

It was then that the Pathans changed their tactics. They decided to first remove Khalid from the equation so that it would be easier to eliminate Dawood. But killing Khalid was totally out of the question because the man was a force of nature and seemed invincible. Their target was only Dawood, and they had to eliminate him to finish his gang. But they knew that Khalid was a hurdle in their paths. He would always protect Dawood. So they needed Khalid out of their hair, which would enable them to net Dawood. If they could ensure a jail term for Khalid, Dawood would be a sitting duck.

The tip-off that led to the seizure of thirty silver bricks and the disclosure of Khalid's name in the smuggling case for the first time was the Pathan's handiwork. Working on a plan, they first squealed on a consignment and then directed the DRI towards Khalid as the kingpin. This had suddenly made the world a smaller place for Khalid and he had to keep looking around all the time.

Among other things, this affected Khalid's wedding plans. Dawood and everyone had decided to make it a lavish affair, but with the police and customs officials looking out for him, this was not meant to be. Some advised that the marriage should be postponed for the time being as '*section garam hai* (the police is hot on their heels).' But this was like conceding defeat to the enemies. The best answer that Dawood could give to the Pathans was to ensure that Khalid got married despite all the external pressure. He decided that nothing should hinder the event.

The marriage took place with all the Pashtun fervour. From the moment the groom entered the shamiana he dissolved into smiles and enjoyed the momentous day.

Marriage brought more sobriety and calmness into Khalid's life. He was always an unlikely member of the mafia community. Despite having migrated to Bombay and living in the city for over a decade, the man did not allow any vice to touch him. Some say he was acting on the advice of a sage: '*Tum us waqt tak badmashi ke badshah rahoge jab tak tum sharab na piyo aur randibaazi na karo* (You will be the king of the Mumbai underworld until the time you shun wine and prostitution).'

Khalid never drank, even if there was intense pressure from his friends. While everyone around him got sozzled, he was seen sipping soft drinks. Similarly, Khalid did not indulge in womanizing and did not go to brothels either.

He had, however, little say in the matter when it came to fellow gang members. Sabir Kaskar was someone who had never wanted to be the head of the gang but, by virtue of being Dawood's elder brother, had this position and the burden fell automatically on him. The entire Dawood–Sabir gang respected him and took his instructions seriously.

Sabir was a Casanova, a poet at heart; he neither paid attention to the business nor did he follow the unforgettable principles of the underworld. Despite having so many enemies baying for his blood, Sabir remained oblivious to impending danger and would keep exposing himself to lurking threats.

Sabir was married to a nice a girl from a respectable family. However, he wore his heart on his sleeve and would keep falling for any good-looking girl. After a while, this weakness he had for women became an obsessive addiction. When Dawood realized that the Pathans were bent on liquidating him and his brother, he decided that they would always be shepherded by bodyguards.

Dawood had understood the intensity of the danger but Sabir remained heedless of the same. Initially, Sabir would inform his men of his whereabouts but he went lax after a while. He believed that he was not answerable to anyone and refused to remain paranoid all his life. Sabir often used to quip in his poetic manner, '*Dil ki dawa sirf daaru aur devi ke dayaar mein hain* (The cure for the heart lies in wine and in the abode of women).'

Sabir's self-assurance proved disastrous not only for him but also resulted in enormous bloodshed in Bombay.

20

The D-Gang

A total of twenty-eight bullets were pumped into Sabir Ibrahim Kaskar. Of these, nine were extracted from his body during the autopsy, while the other nineteen were found embedded in the car seat, floor mat and windows of his Fiat car on 12 February 1981. Sabir had been stealthily ambushed by Amirzada–Alamzeb and four of their minions at Servocare petrol pump in Prabhadevi in central Bombay. He was cornered when he had stopped for refuelling. At the time, Sabir had no bodyguards and was only accompanied by his latest floozy, Chitra, a prostitute from the Congress House brothel.

It was one of those nights when Sabir had sneaked out of their headquarters at Musafir Khana alone, without telling anyone. Hours later, he was found dead in his car, his head on the steering wheel and his wrists slashed to ensure that he bled to death before being hospitalized. Sabir's easy and quick death had made his assailants euphoric.

It is probable that Khalid and Dawood would have discovered Sabir's murder much later, but for Alamzeb and Amirzada's doggedness to complete their unfinished business.

They wanted to kill two birds with one stone. If they had waylaid Sabir, they could also try their luck with Dawood. Perhaps they could catch him unawares. When they stormed Dawood's stronghold at Pakmodia Street, they didn't reckon with Khalid, who had risked his life in the past to save Dawood. Khalid's timely retaliation and presence of mind resulted in Amirzada's injury, and he was eventually abandoned on the street by his cronies who were in a hurry to escape from the spot and save their lives.

Khalid and Dawood swiftly rushed Amirzada to the nearby state-run J.J. Hospital to avoid police complications. They didn't want Amirzada lying dead on their turf. The police would lose no time in implicating them in the murder. At J.J. Hospital, Khalid and Dawood discovered that Sabir's body had also been brought into the casualty ward a few minutes before. While Sabir succumbed to his injuries, Amirzada survived. During his recuperation at J.J. Hospital, Amirzada was booked for Sabir's murder and arrested after his discharge.

In a bid to expedite the hearing on the case, Ibrahim Havildar often tried to seek the help of his old friend A.R. Antulay, who had by then risen in the political ranks to become the chief minister of Maharashtra in 1980. Ibrahim was deeply disturbed by the death of his eldest son. He could not believe that he had been gunned down so brutally when the chief minister of the state was his buddy.

But Antulay could not care less as he himself was embroiled in a massive controversy about cement allotments to select builders who had, in turn, donated towards a public trust fund set up by him. Antulay was firefighting on several fronts, so for him political survival alone was top priority.

Antulay's opponents were baying for his blood, his own ministers were in mutiny and the protracted litigations in the

Bombay High Court kept him anxious and sleepless and on his toes all the time. He was least interested in Ibrahim Havildar or justice for Sabir, who was, after all, a local ganglord.

Eventually, less than a year after Sabir's murder, the high court convicted Antulay of wrongdoing in what was then called 'the cement scandal'. Antulay had to resign as chief minister. For the bereaved father, Ibrahim Havildar, Antulay was a sore disappointment. It made no difference to him that Antulay had lost his political position.

The Kaskar family was distraught. As his father made the rounds of the chief minister's office, Dawood, in deference to his father, did not mention anything about his own revenge formula. Sabir's brutal murder had changed Dawood, the small-time criminal and smuggler, to Dawood, the avenger. For the first time in his life, he felt no qualms about spilling blood and taking a life. He realized that if he allowed the law to take its own course, Amirzada would probably get away with the murder. No, he wanted a life for a life, and, if need be, several lives. He did not care. He wanted to see Amirzada helpless and quaking in fear as death did its deadly dance before his eyes. He waited two long years for Amirzada to seek bail. But the wily Pathan preferred to remain in jail and did not press his lawyer for bail. Imagine, the mighty Pathans were now cowering beneath the petticoats of jailors just to avoid a chit of a boy called Dawood. The Pathans were the first to realize that Dawood was not just a menace but a real, serious threat to their fiefdom in Dongri. The boy was mad and possessed with a burning fire that was unseen and unheard of in the annals of the Bombay mafia.

Dawood reigned at a time when Bombay had an equally deadly police commissioner. Julio Ribeiro, known for his no-nonsense hands-on approach, who later went on to wipe out terrorism from Punjab along with K.P.S. Gill, stood at the helm in Bombay. But not even Ribeiro was able to tame the Bombay mafia. In fact, the mafia members, most of whom came from impoverished backgrounds, ran amuck in the streets of Bombay, with Dawood leading the pack. Between 1982 and 1985, the mafia became bolder and more violent.

The gruesome killing of Sabir was regarded as the turning point for the Bombay mafia. It was after his murder that the mafia began violating all kinds of codes as they crossed personal boundaries and became bloodthirsty. After Sabir's death, the Dawood–Sabir gang decided to coronate Dawood as the chieftain, and the gang was rechristened the 'D-Gang'.

For the two years that Amirzada was safely cocooned inside the precincts of Arthur Road Jail, Dawood used the time constructively to build his gang with the help of Khalid. With Sabir gone, Khalid became indispensable to Dawood. They roped in more Hindus across the city, making the gang more socially inclusive.

Finally, Dawood decided that he would not wait forever for Amirzada's judicial trial. Instead, he would become the judge and executioner in the case. He hatched a daring plan to bump off Amirzada within the premises of the court when he came in for his next hearing before the judge. This was one of the most audacious underworld killings in Bombay. Dawood hired one of the local riff-raffs, David Pardesi, and gave him the contract to shoot Amirzada dead in the sessions court, when he was in the dock.

Pardesi's arrest in the courtroom shootout of Amirzada led to Dawood's arrest from Baroda (now known as Vadodara). Dawood had gone to Porbandar to receive a smuggling consignment when he was arrested by the Baroda Police.

Dawood was lodged at Sabarmati Central Jail, where, it is said, he lived a lavish life by throwing money at the conniving officials.

The Gujarat Police had managed to slap several smuggling cases on him in various cities so as to ensure that he would not be able to get bail easily in an isolated case. They didn't want him to get away from their clutches. These cases, registered at police stations in Surat, Porbandar and Baroda, made him hop from one lock-up to another and often travel long distances by road to appear in various trial courts.

But Dawood, who was born under the zodiac sign of Capricorn, was a determined goat. He never lost sight of his goal and always turned adversity into prosperity. When he realized that the Gujarat Police were dead set on making his life miserable, he turned to make friends with them, so much so that the cops begun to trust him and felt reassured that the man would not conspire to escape from custody.

Actually, Dawood had a very good reason to befriend the Gujarat Police. Though he had managed to kill Amirzada, his other arch-enemy Alamzeb had joined forces with the Gujarat don, Abdul Latif Khan, who at the time was a very powerful bootlegger in the state.

Latif had got David Pardesi shot through his shooter Sharif Khan and was now baying for Dawood's blood. At the Sabarmati jail, Dawood had been alerted about Latif's plans. He knew he was easy prey once he stepped out of jail and was being escorted to other towns in Gujarat.

Initially, whenever Dawood was escorted to the court and back to jail, he was given a police van as protection. But with the passage of time, Dawood noticed that the extra security cover had disappeared. He suspected that the police were making him vulnerable, fair game for his rivals. This changed equation meant that instead of Dawood avenging his brother

Sabir, the vengeance would belong to Alamzeb. Dawood felt vulnerable and more and more like a sitting duck in Gujarat. He did have reason to worry as he was away from his home turf and did not have his human shield, Khalid, by his side to avert any attack on his life.

But the mentor had left an indelible impression in his mind. Dawood had managed to imbibe Khalid's teachings very well. Khalid had taught him the felicity to survive against the heaviest odds: 'Survival is a matter of chutes and ladders. At times life can slide you to the lowest level and dump you in the deepest ebb; however, only a real warrior can turn around this slip to board the escalator to success. And to achieve that aim, he should be always willing to face any eventuality. So much so that if you don't have a screwdriver, then learn to use a hammer to unscrew.' Khalid's lessons never went waste with Dawood.

The proficiency of any pupil depends on how well he can acquire the lessons from his teacher and then add his own two bits to the teaching. Dawood while learning all these aphorisms and strategic lessons also kept improving on them in his own shrewd way.

Khalid had always believed in his own physical prowess, smart thinking and survival skills to emerge out of a tricky situation. He had drilled this mantra into Dawood: 'Nobody but you alone can help yourself in a crisis. You need to have your wits around you and you need loads of courage.'

What Dawood lacked in physical strength, like his teacher, he more than made up for with his unconventional smart thinking and astute moves, which not only helped him survive against all odds but also emerge much stronger, even later in life.

While Khalid never had strong equations with police officers, as the Bombay cops remained parochial in their approach and treated him as an outsider, Dawood, who knew Marathi and hailed from a police background, instantly made friends with the police. He did not hesitate to grease their palms when smooth talking failed. His presence was also very disarming and people didn't realize the powerhouse hidden inside him. He seemed like just another common man who was trying to be affable in the worst of circumstances.

For those policemen who were willing to be on his payroll, Dawood paid them generously to buy their loyalty, while with those who refused to accept money, Dawood assured them 'inside intelligence', which in police terminology means '*andar ki khabar*'. This was the reason that Dawood had very few enemies among the police force, not just in Bombay but even outside the city. While in Gujarat, Dawood nurtured close friendships with them and the cops were always willing to eat out of his hands.

The only vulnerable stretch for Dawood was his trip from Sabarmati Central Jail to the Baroda court and back, which was over 120 km, each side. Dawood realized that he would be totally on his own and needed every trick up his sleeve to survive if he were attacked by his enemies. Sub-inspector Bishnoi, who was only armed with a standard service revolver, was responsible for Dawood's security.

Dawood remained anxious about his safety on the entire drive from Sabarmati to Baroda. But his court appearance was uneventful and they did not face any untoward incident throughout the journey. On their way back, Dawood felt euphoric and even checked into a hotel off Narol highway in Ahmedabad.

Two Dawood aides by the names of Raees and Abdullah were also taken to court for a hearing on the same day. Earlier, Dawood and Sub-inspector Bishnoi were seated on the rear seat, while Raees and Abdullah were in the front seat, one of them driving the Fiat car. But after a break and relaxation at a dhaba in Narol, Dawood decided to switch the seating arrangement.

Dawood asked Raees and Abdullah to shift behind, while he, along with Bishnoi, sat in the front. Dawood then decided to take the wheel and asked Bishnoi, who reluctantly agreed after initially protesting, to sit on the passenger seat. But when Dawood asked Bishnoi to give him his service revolver, the cop put his foot down and refused.

'We are only a few miles from the jail. I am not foolhardy to use the gun against you. If I wanted to escape, I wouldn't have waited until we entered the city limits,' Dawood explained to him. He told Bishnoi that he wanted to keep the gun with him because the assailants would anyway not shoot at Bishnoi because of his uniform but would target Dawood instead.

Sometimes one's worst fears come true. Barely had their car covered a couple of miles towards the Jamalpur Junction (predominantly a Muslim locality and currently still a Muslim ghetto) that Dawood faced his moment of truth.

Jamalpur was known to be Latif's stronghold, and his men, who had been discreetly trailing Dawood since the time he had left Baroda, had planned to corner him in the area. The Jamalpur roads were narrow, the traffic was chaotic and vehicular movement was so haywire that motorists had to literally gnash their teeth to traverse the area.

Alamzeb, his crony Iqbal Bhupat, the big boss, Latif, and his main shooter, Liyaqat Master, who had been trailing Dawood, decided to make their move in this mess of a traffic jam. Liyaqat jumped out of the car, expecting Dawood to be in the rear seat, and came close enough to opening fire at the passengers. Dawood had sensed the car and his pursuers coming closer. He decided to think like Khalid and move the way his teacher would. While Dawood's pursuers expected him to be totally off guard, Dawood had already begun planning his counteroffensive.

Dawood asked Bishnoi to step out of the car and raise an alarm so that the traffic police or any uniformed men around would get drawn towards his cries for help. As instructed, Bishnoi began bellowing and drawing the attention of the uniformed men around. Liyaqat was startled for a moment. But he decided to get closer and shoot at Dawood and then return quickly before anyone could help him.

But Dawood, who had also sneaked out of the car from Bishnoi's side, took cover and trained the gun at Liyaqat Master. Master was mystified when he did not spot Dawood in the car. In his hurry he opened fire at them as a reflex action. Dawood took advantage of this and fired at Liyaqat Master, who lost his balance and fell down. Dawood and Bishnoi both ran towards him. Just a few feet away were two police officers in a cruiser van. The firing and shouts drew their attention and they dashed towards Bishnoi and his friend who was firing. Dawood might have killed Latif's gunman or at least injured him. But Liyaqat realized that the tables had turned against them and he got up and ran towards Latif's car. The hunter had become the hunted. Latif and Alamzeb too did not expect this situation, of Dawood managing to upstage them despite being alone.

The shots and the sight of the two men firing at each other and hurling a volley of bullets at each other had scared other motorists who barely managed to scramble away from these feuding men. Latif found an opening and managed to flee from the spot along with his cronies.

Dawood and Sub-inspector Bishnoi were relieved and happy to remain unhurt in the attack, though Raees and Abdullah had both suffered injuries from Liyaqat's shots.

Dawood had managed to reach the Sabarmati Central Jail precincts safely. Weeks passed and he became increasingly aware that he had to settle scores with Alamzeb soon. The solitude of jail egged him on further to figure out his vendetta. He then formulated a plan to kill Alamzeb. He used his connections and ensured that Alamzeb was killed on the outskirts of Ahmedabad.

The well-planned police encounter of Alamzeb had turned out to be extremely controversial and many questions were raised in its regard. In fact, it had led to a riot-like situation in Ahmedabad, wherein Latif's supporters had forced a bandh in the city in many places. An example of Latif's clout can be seen from the fact that when he was thrown in to jail during the Ahmedabad municipal elections, Latif decided to file his nomination papers from five wards. He managed to win in all five wards despite being in jail.

Dawood was impressed with Latif's hold over Gujarat and realized that even if the latter was Alamzeb's ally, he could still be a useful partner for Dawood in his future ventures. Dawood cleverly avoided locking horns with Latif and kept his enmity limited to the Bombay Pathans.

The stint in jail and being on his own in Gujarat was a learning curve for Dawood. He used his incarceration to good effect. He learned to work around a problem. Alamzeb was killed at the hands of the police even as he was sitting inside a jail cell. Dawood could go to any lengths to avenge his flesh and blood.

Subsequently, after his release from jail and upon being back in Mumbai, Dawood eliminated Samad Khan, which was in retaliation to Samad's assault on his brother Noora. He led a hit squad to kill him in Sikka Nagar on Grant Road. Dawood was relentless in pursuing his enemies and was equally passionate about making pots of money. Sabir's death had cast him among the wolves and he was determined to survive. He realized that money opened many doors, and he wanted to amass as much money as possible. He had also decided to exclude his other brothers from the mafia world. Anis Ibrahim was Dawood's younger brother, who was fascinated with the underworld and wanted to assist Dawood after Sabir's death. But Dawood disapproved and also forced him to migrate to Dubai. It is a different story that Anis was unable to keep away from the D-Gang and became integral to it in the subsequent decades.

Dawood strictly asked Iqbal Kaskar and Nurul Haq, alias Noora, to distance themselves from the underworld. Iqbal was not interested in the violent side of the underworld, while Noora, like Sabir, was a romantic at heart. According to some unconfirmed stories, Noora had composed songs for a few movies under a pseudonym. Dawood's other two brothers Humayun and Mustaqeem were teenagers who were able to focus on their education than on gang activities.

After Sabir's murder, Dawood also realized that none of the money in the world would be enough if he had no access to power. In Gujarat, inside the jail, he had learnt that having access to the corridors of power and policemen opened doors everywhere. If he had to reach the pinnacle, he needed a network of useful contacts. While Dawood's predecessors focused more on seeking acceptability by getting photographed with reigning film stars, Dawood was keen on aligning himself with powerful politicians both in Maharashtra and in Delhi. Eventually, he partnered with both politicians and businessmen in big-ticket projects all over India.

With his family secured and political connections in place, Dawood began to concentrate on his business and gang activities. He then fortified his den at Musafir Khana and gave carte blanche to Khalid to expand their smuggling operations.

21

Musa Ka Ghoosa

The Mumbai underworld has drawn and derived most of its proverbs and idioms from the stories narrated in Muslim religious texts, but these are usually discussed in a different context altogether. Incidentally, these proverbs or figurative expressions were used as allegorical references. For instance, the proverb *'Sulemani keeda'* is an idiom often used to convey that the man is crooked and evil because he has been infected by the gigantic bug of villainy. Now, just a mention of keeda, or bug, will not convey the meaning with any impact. Prophet Suleman, or King Solomon in the Old Testament, was known to have ruled the mightiest, grandest and most powerful kingdom in the world at the time. So, if one wants to convey the enormity of the bug that has bitten a man, the mention of Suleman is made in the expression.

Similarly, another very popular expression, which has its roots in Islamic history, is *'Musa ka ghoosa'*, meaning 'the decisively powerful punch of Moses'. The story goes that Prophet Musa was passing through a bazaar, when he saw his tribesmen and an Israeli locked in a dispute with a native

Copt (Egyptian in the Hellenistic and Roman periods) and was asked to intervene. Musa reluctantly got involved and tried to resolve the matter between the men. However, neither of them was willing to back down. In the heat of the moment, the Copt said something untoward and pounced on Musa for his supposed interference and partiality towards his tribesmen.

Among all the divine messengers, the Holy Quran has mentioned Musa the maximum number of times compared to the others, including the last Prophet Muhammad. Nevertheless, it has also mentioned episodes of Musa's physical prowess and strength as well as his volcanic rage.

Musa was astounded by the man's abrupt aggression and cut him off with a punch, which accidentally landed on the man's face and turned out to be too much for him to handle. The legendary punch was so powerful that the man crashed to the ground and died instantly. The act of throwing a punch was a reflexive movement of self-defence and Musa did not deliberately intend to kill the Copt. The news of the homicide reached the pharaoh, who issued summons for Musa. The army of the pharaoh, meanwhile, had begun searching for the man who was capable of killing another man with a single punch. Consequently, Musa did not want to be incarcerated and had to migrate from Egypt.

There are also other controversial and apocryphal stories mentioned in the Islamic books of Bukhari about Musa punching the angel of death, which made his eyes pop out and made him turn back without extracting his soul. The rage and punch of Musa became iconic in the history of civilization; it was eventually misappropriated by the Bombay underworld who began using it as a proverb. Whenever a man acted in self-defence, or, rather, crushed his adversary into submission, then that reflex was described using the proverbial phrase of *Musa ka ghoosa*.

This phrase is far too fantastic and aspirational in many ways. The dons and gangsters have often used this term, saying, '*Ek Musa ka ghoosa* will suffice.' However, none could achieve this kind of glorious domination in the annals of Bombay's underworld history, except once. Ironically, this prestigious exception also belonged to Dawood's mentor, Khalid, who actually launched an all-pervasive assault to save the life of Dawood's protégé, Shakeel Shaikh, better known as Chhota Shakeel, and Dawood's brother Anis Ibrahim, who had also begun throwing his weight around in the gangland.

Dawood's gang had now grown so big that he also had a group of mercenaries who were referred to as the B-Team; the team that comprised Dawood and Khalid would always be the A-Team, while Anis and Shakeel were at the helm of the B-Team. With the changing gang equations and loyalties, many gangsters were switching sides continuously. One of them was Mehmood Khan, alias Mehmood Kalia, so called because he was dark-complexioned. Kalia had changed sides and joined hands with the Pathans and was now gunning for Dawood and his cronies.

Shakeel had been tasked with the execution of the hit job on Kalia. Kalia's father had a shop in the Tardeo Air-conditioned Market, known as the AC Market, which was regarded as a prestigious business address in the city. However, the market had serpentine corridors and the layout of the entire multistorey plaza was quite confusing for the uninitiated.

When the Shakeel–Anis duo, along with their men, accosted Kalia in the market with the intention of killing him, Kalia, who also had his own men there, managed to get into a duel with them. In the desperate hand-to-hand combat,

Kalia's men began to dominate. Soon, the tables were turned on Shakeel and Anis. Both of them suddenly saw more of Kalia's men joining the skirmish. Kalia's reinforcements made Shakeel's position weaker. They then separated and began using firearms against each other. It was this sudden firing and shooting that created panic among the traders and businessmen. Someone called the police control room about the confrontation in the market.

To add insult to injury, Shakeel also ran out of ammunition and realized his survival was at stake. Displaying great presence of mind, he decided to make his escape from the market, while his aide, who had already seen the balance of scales tilting against Shakeel, managed to get out and make a call to Khalid about Shakeel being in danger.

At the time, Khalid was in Bohri Mohalla and knew that while Anis was Dawood's sibling, Shakeel was also an ace lieutenant of Dawood's and they both could not be left in the lurch. If anything happened to Shakeel, Dawood would find it unbearable. The wound caused due to Sabir's gruesome death was still fresh. Another such incident, after such a short interval, would completely shatter Dawood, who was still lodged inside Sabarmati Central Jail. Khalid's true test of friendship lay in him acting on his own and doing whatever Dawood would do if he were around. In a lightning hurry, Khalid, who was dressed in a kurta and lungi, did not even think of changing his clothes, immediately opened his hidden enclosure in the wall, grabbed an AK-47 and a few rounds and dashed towards his car.

As the roaring, impatient Fiat, jumping all signals and cutting off several lanes, dangerously zoomed out of Pakmodia Street and made an exit from Nagpada coming out on to Bellasis Road, it got shoved aside by a police vehicle that had come ahead of it. The police jeep was in a tearing hurry and was responding to the control room's dispatches of panic about a firing incident inside the AC Market. Initially, Khalid thought of overtaking the jeep, but on second thought he decided to take advantage of a police vehicle rushing at full speed with its whirling orange lights and blaring klaxons and sirens. Soon, Khalid realized that perhaps this police jeep too was headed to the same spot and he asked his driver to stick close to the blue-coloured jeep with the yellow-orange stripes so that they could reach the spot faster and without any hurdles.

In the meanwhile, Shakeel realized that the gang of pursuers behind him was only increasing. Whichever corridor he was moving into, whether at a higher floor or lower, he found his enemies to be always behind him. Soon, they were crawling on all storeys and had also begun manning both the lifts.

However, after a lot of ducking and dodging, Shakeel and Anis both managed to reach the ground floor. The building did not have a wide portico. So, the distance between the entrance to the building and the main gate was barely 50 metres. They thought that if they managed to cross the main gate then they would be safe as they would easily be able to melt into the crowd outside. But Kalia's men saw them from afar and started rushing towards them. For Shakeel and Anis, the gate was in sight and within reach. They had to just beat their pursuers to the main gate. The distance was just 50 metres but it must have felt like the longest 50-metre sprint of the duo's life while they were being stalked by death. Though being chased by half-a-dozen men, they were still quite confident of escaping.

Their self-assuredness was only growing with each step towards the gate. But, suddenly, they stopped in their tracks. They were horror-struck to see six more men materialize from nowhere and stand like a wall at the main gate, while one of them closed the wrought-iron gate behind them. This seemed like a dead end for them. They both stopped at a distance from the gate, sweating profusely, panting furiously, with the realization that they had lost today writ large on their faces. Soon their pursuers too came close and halted behind them.

Anis and Shakeel were surrounded from all sides. While they were totally unarmed, their adversaries seemed to be well-equipped with iron rods, crowbars, Rampuri knives and choppers. Now, every ticking second was a bonus for them as they could see their death inch closer. They were so unequal in number that putting up a fight was unimaginable. They were just waiting for their enemies to attack—a ruthlessly painful and excruciatingly slow attack.

At that very instance, a white Fiat came to a screeching halt outside the gate and from it emerged a raging expletive-spouting man. He had an AK-47 in his hand and seemed to be angry enough to spray the bullets at whoever came in his sight.

In fact, as police officers who witnessed the scene later recalled, this seemed to be a scene straight out of a Bollywood potboiler of that era, where the hero showed up right in the nick of the time when his friend was on the verge of almost getting killed at the hands of goons.

The police jeep that was ahead of the Fiat was about to halt, when the cops turned behind to see the screeching car. The police driver thought that he should avoid a rear collision and moved ahead, but in the scramble the jeep climbed the divider and crossed over the road to the opposite side. A police jeep gone awry will always block the free flow of traffic. The smooth plying of vehicles on both sides of the road came to a grinding halt. As the policemen trooped out of the jeep to restore some semblance of order, they had to immediately duck for cover. They saw a giant of a man gone berserk with a big gun spewing bullets all over the place. A stray bullet, or even a ricochet, could mean death for them. Better safe than sorry was what the policemen were obviously thinking.

Khalid had flung open the gate with one hand and with the other was holding the Kalashnikov rifle, which was a rare sight in those days. During one of their smuggling expeditions, Dawood had managed to get two AK-47s smuggled into Bombay along with gold and other contraband. Dawood had kept one for himself and given the other to Khalid. In the Bombay underworld, until then, only these two men owned a pair of these guns, with none of the other gangsters being able to lay their hands on the weapon.

In fact, even Hindi films did not show AK-47s on screen. It was only in the 1990s and post the 1993 serial blasts in Bombay that these rifles were sighted frequently on and off the screen. Many a killing in the city was orchestrated allegedly through AK-47s, especially by Dawood's duo Sunil Sawant, alias Sautya, and Subhash Singh Thakur.

Despite all that anger and rage brewing inside him, Khalid had not lost control over his senses. He knew very well that a Kalashnikov is regarded as one of the most lethal weapons in the world. Also, it is known to be an assault weapon and not a defence weapon, so one is supposed to use it with utmost discretion. The gun, if mishandled, is capable of mass killings. With clinical precision, Khalid opened fire on the people who had surrounded Shakeel; he was cautious and aimed below the waist and on the legs, not on the torso. This ensured that the volley of bullets was used as a deterrent and a weapon to frighten and not kill.

As someone later said, that day, Khalid's wild bellowing persona at the dramatic scene would have been enough to scare off the goons. The speeding car, police jeep and blazing gun were a bit of an overkill. In no time, the toughies who had surrounded Shakeel realized that they should escape to safety. Khalid took Shakeel by the arm and got inside the car. Even before the police could move and take charge, Khalid had stormed the place, rescued his friends and decamped—all in the blink of an eye.

Seething with fury and frustration, Kalia decided to exact his revenge in a gruesome manner. Kalia, along with his top aide, Ranjeet, made a '*sutli* bomb' and decided to hurl it at Khalid to kill him. However, they had not conducted their recce well enough and so, when they reached the spot, they did not try to verify whether the burly man reclining against the car was indeed Khalid. They just saw someone in a kurta and lungi, with a large back, and presumed it was him. It turned out to be someone else. The bomb, too, turned out be a dud and was only able to injure the man. Khalid decided to settle scores with Kalia for this attack, but he was never able to lay his hands on Kalia, who had by then escaped to Dubai.

Shakeel had a narrow escape that day and survived because of the sheer courage of Khalid. Till today, he remains grateful to him. It has been over three decades since then, but even today, if there is a slight conflict between the two, Shakeel, in deference to Khalid, invariably backs off—something that he never does for anyone except his boss, Dawood.

Retired ACP Malgi, who had long ago tried to help and sponsor Dawood's education, later recalled that Khalid's attack that day had been devastating, just like a *Musa ka ghoosa*, the likes of which was never seen again.

22

The Gold 'Wave'

The area boasted the densest mangroves in the coastal belt of Jampore Beach in Gujarat. People would be reluctant to enter it even during the daytime. But these eight to ten men, some desperados from Mumbai, and other burly locals from Vapi and Bhilad in Gujarat had stepped into these thickets in the wee hours of the morning. They were barefoot and found walking in the marshy quicksand a big challenge.

But they kept walking tenaciously for over 2 km. As they kept walking further, the level of sea water kept rising higher and higher. Finally, they reached a spot where the water levels were higher than chest level. The men gathered in a tight circle and waited. After some time, one of them noticed a motorboat a little distance away. The boat killed its engine and waited a while. The men on the boat then beamed a torchlight in the direction of the waiting bunch. In response, these men shone a torchlight back. The boat edged closer.

The men on the boat, upon reaching the group, asked for the code word. Those were the days when codes were pre-decided and with the mere exchange of a few words, precious cargo worth lakhs of rupees was handed over. The codes ranged from funny to ridiculous and absurd. Sometimes it was foul expletives. At other times it said things like '*naak mein rassi* (rope in the nose)'. The huge consignment of RDX intended for the 1993 serial bombings changed hands just because the recipients had used the code words 'We are from Bombay'.

These men were handed several jackets and asked to tightly button up. Each one of them wore three to four jackets one on top of the other. The motorboat, after handing over the jackets, turned around and left. These men then once again began the arduous walk back towards the shore.

Vapi, Daman and Jampore Beach were some of the favourite haunts of smugglers for landing gold in Gujarat. Gold was brought to Gujarat and Raigad, and it was these coasts that were considered safe by smugglers as they were not exposed to surveillance or vigilance by the customs authorities.

This walk through the mangroves was quite difficult, risky and fraught with several dangers. It was painfully slow and those walking were vulnerable to getting caught as the whole exercise took several hours to execute. The slightest carelessness or slip-up could cause a massive intelligence leak, which would alert the authorities. As it was a tedious and slow process of going into the waters and waiting and then again taking the same amount of time to return, the authorities could net them easily if they found out.

Once the team got back to the shore, they would empty the jackets from the gold biscuits and open the hidden cavities in the jeep where they stashed the gold to be transported to Bombay's markets. There were so many chinks in the whole plan that they could easily get busted. The smugglers' syndicate needed to devise a plan that would ensure the elimination of the risk and make the cargo landing convenient without depending on so many men.

Khalid was trying to devise new ways and means to actually improve on the logistics and transportation of the gold consignment from Dubai to India, which resulted in enhanced security for the smuggled gold in its journey to reach Bombay's coasts. Since the risks were minimized, Khalid ensured that the turnover was increased and revenue maximized. Actually, Khalid had applied simple mathematics and the basic laws of commerce to generate more business and make bigger profits, even if there was a ceiling on the margin ratio.

Each gold biscuit that the Bombay smugglers procured from Dubai cost Rs 150 per *tola* (10 gm). Each biscuit weighed 10 tolas (100 gm), costing somewhere around Rs 1500. By the time it reached Bombay's shores through boats or launches, greasing the palms of the customs officers and landing in the gang's warehouse, the gold biscuit's value increased to Rs 300 per tola, or 3000 per biscuit. The smugglers used to keep a margin of 25 per cent on the consignment when it was sold to the gold traders in south Bombay. So, every tola of smuggled gold was sold at Rs 375.

The gold traders faced the maximum risk with regard to hiding the gold from the customs and the police and showing it as legit procurement. The big buyers and traders then passed it on to small traders and then the dealers' chain down the line. This escalated the gold prices in the 1980s and the yellow metal, or *peela*, was sold at retail in the range of Rs 1375 per tola. Despite all the hurdles, smugglers found gold to be the most lucrative and profitable contraband smuggled into India from Dubai.

On the smugglers' speedboats, which the gold cartel organized from Dubai, gold biscuits were packed in jackets. Each jacket had over 100 biscuits in various pockets, which means there was 10 kg of gold in each jacket, with every speedboat carrying between seventy to eighty jackets stacked discreetly, depending on capacity. In terms of money and investment, each speedboat was valued at a minimum of Rs 2–3 crore in the 1980s. So, every seizure meant a massive loss in millions for the mafia.

One of the smartest moves in this entire gamut of operations was Khalid's ingenious strategy, which emphasized that the speedboats carry the gold, cross the international waters of Dubai Creek and reach the territorial waters in the Indian seas, all without getting intercepted.

The DRI and customs motorboats start patrolling in the Indian territorial waters around 12 nautical miles, or 22.2 km into the sea. Beyond the territorial waters or transboundary limits, as per the maritime delimitation, the naval vessels monitor the intrusion of enemy vessels or spy boats breaching sea borders. While the navy and the DRI were already monitoring traffic in the sea, the Indian government added another line of surveillance by introducing the Indian Coast Guard in 1978. A dhow or motor launch carrying gold had to cross these three sentinels of surveillance and security, the navy, the DRI and the Coast Guard, supplemented by the boats of Yellow Gate Police, Station of the Bombay Police, before it reached the Indian coast.

The agencies' main leitmotif was national security and vigilance against illegal intrusions, but they ended up intercepting a lot of smuggling boats. Many a times, innocuous and harmless fishing trawlers would get hauled up by the agencies. The solution provided by the government for amnesty to these fishermen was to get their boats listed with the agencies and provide them with some kind of document, which later became known as a fishing licence and which helped establish their credentials as bona fide fishermen.

This four-tier security system could be breached only by the fishing trawlers, which, legally, were allowed to move freely. Fishing is a business of chance and opportunity. Sometimes they net a huge amount of fish in their nylon nets, while at other times the catch is disappointing.

It is for this reason that fishermen often sail into deeper reaches of the sea and farther limits of international waters, crossing into the territories of neighbouring countries like Pakistan or Sri Lanka. Often the navy of these countries chases the Indian fishermen and also has skirmishes with them. Occasionally, many fishermen are also arrested on the suspicion of spying by Pakistan.

The fishermen's community is highly superstitious about netting a big catch and heavily ascribe their success to luck and good fortune. So, in this scenario, if someone approaches them and promises them a stable income regardless of the amount of catch in the open sea, it is difficult to resist such a lucrative offer.

Khalid had managed to persuade a few big fishermen with trawlers to venture out into the open seas and cross the territorial waters. Once they were beyond the watch of the four-tier security patrol of the Indian agencies, Khalid's men would get their speedboats close to the fishing trawlers. Khalid managed to load the gold consignment on to the speedboats from Dubai and then transfer the contraband into fishing boats some 30–40 km into the high seas. The whole transfer of goods was done within a few minutes and without alerting the eagle eyes of any kind of vigilance agency.

These fishing boats can surreptitiously hide the gold-laden jackets below their cache of fish and bring them to Indian shores safely. These boats can then unload the gold at Versova, Vashi, Juhu, Gorai and other beaches in Bombay. It was a pragmatic and simple arrangement that had defied all security and opposition and ensured that the gold always reached the city. Sometimes, Khalid also used fishermen from southern India and unloaded consignments in Madras (now known as Chennai), Mangalore and through jetties at Kerala.

This was an unbeatable masterstroke, which would only maximize the gang's earnings and give them the upper hand in gold smuggling. Soon, this method of beating the law became all the rage in the smuggling world. The Dawood gang started to make a killing in the seas.

In the meanwhile, Dawood was cleared of all COFEPOSA charges by the Gujarat court in 1983 and returned to Bombay like a triumphant don. His gang had definitely proved its supremacy in smuggling after liquidating their detractors in the Pathan clan.

Dawood may have been paying less attention to the logistics and intricacies of smuggling, but he was steadily growing in influence. The connections and nexus Dawood made with politicians, the police and customs officials were invaluable to him and were being worked upon for future use and troubleshooting.

Khalid briefed Dawood about the business and how he had managed to increase the profit margin through his deft handling of vessels at sea. Dawood heard the whole strategy and was mighty impressed with his game plan. Then Khalid proposed that Dawood make a visit to Galadari in Dubai. Dawood could not believe that Khalid was so transparent that he did not have any problem in introducing Dawood to his partner who was one of the most influential and powerful businessmen in Dubai.

Within a few days, Dawood and Galadari were seated opposite each other. Dawood was overawed by the opulence of Galadari's multibillion-dollar empire; he had never seen such staggering fortune and affluence. Dawood had seen Haji Mastan and Bashu Dada closely and often spoke about their wealth with exclamatory expressions, but on that day he realized that they were not close to being even the errand boys for this filthy rich Arab.

Both Galadari and Dawood met each other with extreme warmth and cordiality as Khalid was the common link between them. They had both heard legendary things about each other, which spiked their admiration further. However, what the two of them did not realize was that there was mutual dislike and disapproval right in the first meeting and the vibes did not match. Incidentally, Khalid was totally clueless about this disconnect between two of his closest friends.

Once in Dubai, Dawood met with Pakistani syndicates as well and hobnobbed with them at various levels. Dawood had a certain earthiness about him and he realized that his rapport and comfort level were much smoother with Pakistani smugglers, including the Bhatti brothers, Chhota Zikar, Bada Zikar and others. The Pakistani smugglers were keen on a willing and hungry Indian partner, and Dawood fit the bill. Soon, Dawood and the Pakistani syndicate began discussing plans to smuggle gold and other contraband from Dubai.

Khalid and Dawood returned from Dubai and began pushing their business to new levels of intensity and volume. They both were heads of the Bombay syndicate, and most of the rules of the group were drafted by Khalid himself as he had a commerce and business studies background. The basic principles of the syndicate were that anyone can do business, contribute money, invite venture capital, rope in sponsors, collaborate with anyone and do anything that resulted in the business's promotion and profit augmentation. A part of the profit margin would be invested in the syndicate's coffers.

So Khalid could not force Dawood to exclusively do business with Galadari and not associate with any Pakistanis. In fact, Khalid never actually anticipated a scenario where Galadari and Dawood would not get along well with each other. But, at the same time, he could neither object nor insist on them becoming business partners and collaborators. However, Khalid was not exactly in a celebratory mood about Dawood's new-found affiliations or friendship with the Pakistanis.

Khalid, in his experience and foresight, understood that soon the Bombay syndicate would be plagued by internal strife and competition, which is the bane of any organization, often weakening it and undermining its growth. Dawood was, by instinct, an impulsive man and felt that foresight had no room in business. It later became evident that Dawood's impetuous decisions proved too costly for him in unimaginable ways. As Gautama Buddha once said: 'Your worst enemy cannot harm you as much as your own unguarded thoughts.'

23

An Amicable Parting

It landed like a huge punch on his sternum. Khalid was incredulous with disbelief. The news shook him to his core.

'*Maal phir pakda gaya* (The goods have been seized again).'

'*Arré, dekh kar batao, confirm karo, hamara hi hai ya koi aur boat hai* (Please check again, confirm again, whether it is our boat or someone else's).'

'*Bhai aapka hi maal hai* (The goods are certainly yours).'

Unbelievable.

Impossible.

Such news and occurrences were normally anticipated in the smuggling business. The interception of a motorboat with a hundred or eighty jackets of gold once in a year was considered an inevitable loss and was written off in the books of the syndicate, with the loss normally shared among the partners and sponsors.

The syndicate worked on the margin of making enough neat profits from the nine shipments, so if they lost on the tenth one, they would find the grief acceptable. Gold smuggling, in those days, was the business of a chosen few who had the capacity to hedge their risks, handle losses and have the appetite for managing financial downturn in the business.

This particular call was different. It was no routine call of customs interception of their gold-laden dhow. This was the fifth such seizure of a gold consignment in a row. The amount of loss with each boat seized by the authorities was mind-boggling. The seizure of boat after boat and the incessant losses were heartbreaking and spine-chilling for everyone. Personally, Khalid was badly shaken by these developments. He had a vague sense of foreboding that someone was ratting on them systematically.

There was no way that the Indian customs had suddenly become so competent, vigilant and dexterous that they could score such consecutive successes. It was not a coincidence. This seemed like a well-planned and persistent enemy action with a clear-cut agenda to destabilize the syndicate.

Khalid decided to make a trip to Dubai and talk to Wahab Galadari. Perhaps he would come up with some solution. Galadari was an astute businessman and was generally able to solve Khalid's business complications in a jiffy. In fact, his company, A.W. Galadari Holdings, was considered to be the third-largest Arab investor in Singapore.

However, the last few months were equally turbulent and traumatic for Galadari too. Business experts and economists believe that he secretly harboured the desire to become the gold king of the world. The Indian media had already dubbed him 'Goldfinger', one of the most Machiavellian villains of James Bond movies. Galadari was just too much in love with the yellow metal. During his youth he used to smuggle gold in dhows and would even travel till Bombay's coast—a feat which none of the Pakistani smugglers could ever replicate, or even wanted to.

Galadari passionately believed that the gold that first got him his millions was the key to increasing his multibillion-dollar empire. In February 1983, Galadari had launched an ambitious business plan of gold and silver futures, much like the New York one. Galadari could never believe that this would eventually turn out to be his Waterloo.

The idea behind trading in futures commodity is protecting the traders against the fluctuations in the market for a specific time period. This idea was floated way back in the early 19th century for rapidly shifting the prices of coffee plantations. This was later used for rice and wheat prices in most of the agrarian economies across the world, including India. In the Middle East, futures trading was being used for oil trading so as to prevent petrol prices from skyrocketing.

Inspired by the international markets and rising commerce, Galadari began using futures for gold and silver to hedge the risk of traders. It was a grandiose plan and needed the full support of the international markets. However, he received a lukewarm response for his schemes from the business community in the UAE. Soon, Galadari begin incurring massive losses in futures. The trade and commodity exchanges begin seeking the reimbursement of their losses. Galadari kept ignoring these escalating losses and, moreover, stubbornly continued to do business in gold and underwriting the risks of his dealers to his account. The business proposition protected his buyers but undermined his own wealth.

Galadari was pleased to see Khalid again. He met him with the same warmth and cordiality as usual. They discussed the declining business prospects for hours and also expressed concerns over the unfavourable market conditions. Galadari's plummeting fortunes, spiralling debts, disastrous business decisions and sense of complacency in the face of dire crisis had blunted his sharpness. After hearing out the travails of Khalid, Galadari asked him to continue the smuggling and face the losses with gumption. 'We shall overcome this together, inshallah,' he said reassuringly.

Khalid was surprised at the older man's stoic resilience and his sagacity in bearing the losses against all odds. With encouragement from Galadari, Khalid decided to persevere and continue smuggling.

The plans for the sixth trip of the motorboat were kept a secret. Khalid did not want anyone besides Dawood, himself and Galadari to know. Khalid believed that his goods were being seized and his boats getting intercepted because too many people knew about the operation. There were suspicions that one of the people involved in the project on either side was playing the snitch and tipping off the agencies.

Absolute secrecy and working on a need-to-know principle in smuggling ensures that the intelligence is never shared and the agencies never find out about the existence or transport of the gold. Khalid took every possible precaution in the smuggling world and he also brought his own pragmatic wisdom into play. He was confident of getting through this time.

But the sixth time too Khalid's goods got confiscated. The motorboat was surrounded in the high seas. The moment it entered India's territorial waters, the agencies swooped down on the boat and seized the gold consignment. When the call came, Khalid felt beads of sweat appearing on his forehead. He felt weak when he replaced the phone receiver in its cradle.

This could not simply be a streak of misfortune and bad luck. Khalid wondered about Dawood's gold shipment loaded by the Pakistani smugglers reaching the desired landing spots without any hindrance or incidents. In the last few months, only Galadari's gold had been seized. The principal losses belonged to the Galadari–Khalid combine and partially to Dawood. On the other hand, the Pakistani syndicate's gold partnership belonged exclusively to Dawood and only part of it to Khalid. There clearly seemed to be some diabolical conspiracy aimed at wiping out Galadari and his share in the market. Once a giant like him, who was considered a golden whale in the ocean of smuggling, was eliminated, the seas would be totally open for the other players. It seemed to be the Pakistani syndicate's well-thought-out stratagem to establish their hegemony.

The consistent seizure of every motorboat was a major setback to Khalid's business plans and a financial blow to his sponsor, Galadari. But little did Khalid know that Galadari was bleeding not just on the smuggling front but in most of his other business ventures as well.

The London-based auditing firm Peat, Marwick, Mitchell & Co. (which was later merged and is now known as KPMG) had stated that A.W. Galadari would not survive unless it closed certain unprofitable businesses immediately and also sold off some top-notch properties in New York and London, including his penthouses.

According to a report, Galadari's overdraft facility with his own bank, Union Bank of the Middle East, exceeded over 100 million dollars. This was reported to the UAE government, which had to step in to curb the spiralling crisis. Inquisition and monitoring bodies were immediately set up to resolve and redress the critical mess in the banking sector.

Wahab's brothers Rashid and Latif rushed to their sibling's rescue but could do little as his risk-taking abilities had gone beyond limits. The financial abyss that Galadari had sunk himself in was simply too deep for him to be rescued out of.

Both the brothers had to sell off Galadari's property development projects in Singapore and divest his stakes from other companies. Galadari was hurtling towards penury at an accelerated pace, and despite his brother's help and the UAE government's lenient attitude his troubles only got compounded.

The usually flamboyant and media-savvy Galadari went into seclusion. He cut down on meeting everyone and avoided public appearances and gatherings. For him, the end seemed to be nigh. Since his stupendous rise to power barely two decades ago he had never expected his downfall to occur in such a vicious manner.

Political experts and stalwarts of the Dubai market aver that some of Galadari's undoing was precipitated by the local Arabs (or Watnis), who had been hostile towards him since the beginning as he was a naturalized Arab of Iranian origin and not a native of the UAE. So the 'son of the soil' issue was not just flagrant talk but a resurgent movement slowly assuming endemic proportions globally.

However, in November 1983, Galadari was removed from the chairmanship of his own bank and most of his properties, including his Hyatt Regency complex, were attached to recover the debt. He was eventually declared bankrupt and was also detained for a few months by the government.

Galadari sequestered himself from the world and started leading a frugal life on the subsistence allowance provided to him by the UAE government. He was reduced to a shadow of his former self, though both his brothers continued living opulently. In fact, Latif also visited India and, through his shrewd manipulative subterfuges, enabled a few legal cases to be dropped against his family.

On account of Galadari's bankruptcy and retirement from active business, Khalid lost a bulwark of support in the UAE, and though he knew the Pakistani smugglers quite well, he still did not want to do business with them. Khalid was also sceptical of them and their motives. Despite his ancestors hailing from Pakistan, Khalid felt that aligning with them was tantamount to working against India.

Were the Pakistanis behind all the interceptions? Did they orchestrate the whole sordid drama in the high seas, and did they plan on repeating this ploy to push Khalid into a quagmire of losses and debt? Was this their ruthless way of bringing him to his knees and forcing him to work with their syndicate? Khalid had never found himself so perplexed and confused.

Khalid's quandary worsened further when one day Dawood stepped into the office and saw Khalid in a pensive mood. After the initial pleasantries and small talk, Dawood initiated the conversation, '*Bhai, hum log alag ho kar dhanda karte hain* (Let us part ways and do business separately).'

'*Kyun, kya hua* (Why, what happened)?' Khalid asked in bewilderment; he felt that Dawood was not serious.

'I think if we both run two gangs separately, it would be great for us. We would have two friends on different thrones calling the shots. *Akhhe Bombay mein hum dono hi honge phir* (It will then be only the two of us in all of Bombay),' said Dawood.

Khalid dismissed the idea of the dissolution of their partnership. But Dawood's suggestion had added fuel to the fire. It set him thinking. Subsequently, Khalid gathered that Dawood was getting influenced by the Pakistani smugglers. They were trying to plant seeds of separation in Dawood's mind. '*Tumhari gang toh Khalid chala raha hai, tumhari kahan chalti hai iss gang mein* (It is Khalid who is running the gang, you have no say),' was the chatter that reached Khalid's ears.

Khalid was seething with silent rage and fury at the temerity of the Pakistanis. Khalid was the one who had introduced them to Dawood, and now they were trying to effect a split between the two friends for monetary gains. He did not want to separate from Dawood and wanted him to continue to be his friend and business partner. Khalid desperately wanted to make his gold smuggling from Dubai work.

But Khalid still wanted to struggle and prove his mettle in this crisis. He was the man who had singularly been responsible for making gold smuggling a highly lucrative business. He had introduced so many safety measures and smart methods to augment the profits at every level. But he hadn't been able to figure out how things had gone so horribly wrong. Not once but half-a-dozen times in a row had his gold been confiscated, and this had not happened in his over-twelve-year career in smuggling. But Dawood, on the other hand, was managing to engage in all kinds of risky ventures with the Pakistanis, and he was getting it right all the time.

The *kachra peti*, or dustbin line, was so fraught with risk, but Dawood was a pioneer and managed to continue smuggling gold successfully through it. The idea was simple: a passenger would carry the gold packet in a chocolate box or a box like that of a tape recorder, radio or similar such items. Just before the green channel (customs clearance), the passenger would slyly drop the box in a dustbin on the way and move towards customs declaration. The passenger would be trailed by an airport employee who would pick up the box, include it in his own belongings and carry it out of the airport when his duty hours ended that day. He would later deliver the box at the instructed address.

This 'kachra peti line' worked very well and Dawood managed to smuggle in small consignments of gold biscuits without any hassles. Despite so many plausible goof-ups, nothing happened and the gold kept coming in. Khalid was mystified at Dawood's uncanny and consistent streak of success, and his clever work in dodging the authorities.

Khalid remained restless and perturbed for days at his incessant losses and often spent sleepless nights in search of a solution that remained elusive. Finally, one morning Khalid woke up with clarity. He decided to smuggle in one last shipment of gold from Dubai. This would be the decisive consignment. It would establish whether he should continue working with the Dawood–Pakistani syndicate or find an alternative option. On that day in April 1984 Khalid may have had an epiphany of sorts.

He again ordered gold from Dubai. As per usual, he organized the jackets and had them loaded with gold biscuits. The launch started from Dubai at a predetermined time. Khalid did not give any details to anyone. It was a closely guarded secret, more fiercely protected even than Chinese codes, which are the most secretive in the world. However, Khalid made it a point to let Dawood know all the details, the vessel's description, the landing dates and other such relevant information.

As expected, the boat was accosted by the patrolling boats of the customs department. It was the seventh consignment that had been caught by the DRI sleuths. Khalid's suspicion was proved right.

As Dawood sauntered into the office that day, the atmosphere was mournfully grim. Khalid, who had remained awake all night, had made up his mind. He inhaled deeply and with a cold audible sigh said, 'Dawood, you were right, we should separate. It is better to part as friends than to continue as competitors or rivals.'

Dawood nodded and kept looking at Khalid, as if searching in his mentor's eyes for explanations. Khalid shielded his eyes to prevent them from expressing the pain he felt. It was like a raw stab wound. He felt that had Dawood really stabbed him, he would have fared better. This was worse. He had not felt so much pain even after the Bashu episode. The knot in his chest was tightening; he felt like he was choking. But Dawood, his protégé, would never know. Khalid would not reveal his pain to the person who caused it. He wanted to summon a smile but for some reason his facial muscles did not cooperate. *The Pathans are a doughty race, I will tide over this too,* Khalid thought to himself.

Years after the incident, Khalid found out how the whole chain of betrayals had played out. He realized that the information leak was the handiwork of a Dubai-based agent by the name of Ibrahim, who was working at the behest of the Pakistani syndicate.

In the underworld, the separation of erstwhile friends and business associates always ends with bloodshed and violence. Internecine feuds between two former cronies often lead to a battle for supremacy. However, this was the only parting in the Bombay mafia that was amicable and took place without an exchange of a heated word or a foul expletive, leave alone violence.

Khalid and Dawood's friendship concluded peacefully. It has been over thirty-five years since they parted ways. And to this day Khalid and Dawood are friends.

24

'Never Get Caught'

Khalid was a great teacher, and Dawood, the quick learner that he was, picked up a lot of important lessons from the former. In terms of business, Dawood learnt the ropes of smuggling, mega-scale operations, the ways of legitimatizing illegal income and various other essentials of the smuggling tradecraft. Khalid had also taught him the art of survival in street skirmishes and imbibed in him the techniques of cerebral warfare. This multidimensional training had given Dawood an aura of invincibility. Dawood felt he had learnt all that was to be learnt and could make no mistakes.

A talented and successful protégé always learns much more than what he is taught by his mentor. Dawood was like a sponge who absorbed the minutest details of Khalid's instructions and planning. But he focused more on money and less on the finer traits of character. Thus, pristine values like loyalty, self-sacrifice, giving precedence to others and other such lofty morals seemed to be of little or no importance to Dawood. Khalid, who deeply believed in these values, had tried to instil them in his protégé, who chose to pick up only those which served his purpose.

Psychologists opine that every individual youth or character is actually an offshoot or sum total of his or her childhood. A person can be better understood if the circumstances of his formative years are analysed in the proper perspective. Dawood's childhood had been one of abject poverty and suffering, of humiliation and bitterness heaped on his family from all quarters. Often all twelve of them, including his parents and siblings, starved and had only one meal a day. Following Head Constable Ibrahim Kaskar's suspension, things had become even worse for the whole family.

This fashioned Dawood's psychology; he saw his mother and father struggling to bring up their large brood. Their struggles and depression shook him from the inside. While the eldest son, Sabir, found solace in poetry and beautiful girls, Dawood remained restless. In subsequent years, Dawood became obsessed with money and the power that came with it. His lust for power and money made him avaricious and insecure. In his quest to dominate and become rich, he forgot an important principle of life—the significance of human ties beyond blood relations.

People often follow the path of their closest friends. Dawood grew up with Jenabai Daruwali and imbibed lessons in manipulating people around her. Jenabai was a friend of Dawood's mother, Amina, and was addressed as 'Maasi' (aunt) by the whole Kaskar clan. Jenabai was an informer for the Bombay crime branch, who had made a sizeable fortune through bootlegging.

A snitch leads several complex lives; for survival, people often have to be misled, deceived and used for the bigger objectives in life. Before Dawood began spending time with

Khalid, his young mind had already been corrupted by Jenabai and her dubious dealings. Dawood was quick to learn the ropes; he successfully applied all that he was taught in his future ventures, smuggling and politics.

Jenabai has been extensively profiled in my book *Mafia Queens of Mumbai*, which details how her clout with the police and ganglords had made her a powerful figure in the underworld. Jenabai taught everyone around her that 'there are no real friends or real enemies in the world beyond family; everyone is useful and has come into this world for a specific purpose.'

Since his teenage years, Dawood had befriended people with an ulterior motive and then discarded them once they had served their purpose. Right from the retired ACP Burhan Malgi who had supported Dawood in his school days to other cops who came into his life, all of them were just the means to a particular end. Dawood applied the same fundamentals while dealing with the members of the mafia. From Bashu Dada to Haji Mastan to Karim Lala and other stalwarts of the Bombay underworld, Dawood wanted to topple everyone and reign supreme.

In fact, the oldies like Karim Lala got so rattled at one point of time by Dawood's vengeful campaign against the Pathan syndicate that he travelled to the holy city of Mecca to call a truce with Dawood. Karim Lala was close to Ibrahim Kaskar but he could never figure out Dawood. But in Mecca, at the Masjidul Al-Haram, in the precincts of the Holy Kaaba, Karim Lala and Dawood both hugged and cried for a long time and renewed their old bond. It was only after this that Dawood withdrew his onslaught against the Pathans. The underworld still remembers the legendary humiliation of Haji Mastan and Bashu Dada in public at the hands of Dawood Ibrahim.

Soon after Dawood's association with Khalid, his syndicate grew from strength to strength. Dawood learnt the logistics and economics of smuggling. He had accumulated enough wealth and influence that he could have remained contented and retired the way others from his era had done. However, Dawood got locked in a battle of one-upmanship. Every act was a competition for him and everyone was an adversary if they didn't kowtow to him. People had to come to him through sheer volition or under duress. He also used pressure, politics and chicanery when the need arose.

Dawood firmly believed that to make an omelette, one needs to break the egg. In Dawood's universe, if you want to not only survive but marvellously succeed in the underworld, then you must decimate your equals or even those who aspire to be your equals. In fact, Dawood—who has never read *Chanakya Neeti* and would not know of the world-famous philosopher, economist and jurist's strategy of *saam* (suggest), *daam* (buy), *dand* (punish) and *bhed* (disrupt)—believed this aggression would fuel his master plan for success. The idea was simple: break everyone either through money or threats.

Dawood began the execution of his plan in the most ruthless manner. The foremost weapons that he used were dand and daam. Dawood began punishing his enemies either through his men or through the system. To this end, he began exploiting the weaknesses of his enemies by bribing government officials.

The systematic elimination of Pathan gangs—comprising Alamzeb, Amirzada, Samad Khan and Mehmood Kalia—meant finishing off every threat in his climb to success. While Amirzada and Samad were killed through hired killers, Alamzeb and Mehmood were killed in dubious police encounters. Mehmood was killed right after his arrival from Dubai outside the car park of Santa Cruz Airport, while Alamzeb was killed by the Baroda Police in Gujarat. Later, Rama Naik, who was ganglord Arun Gawli's close confidante, was also killed in a police encounter in Chembur.

It is still debatable whether the Bombay Police and customs officials used Dawood, or whether he used them. The collaboration with government officials made him shrewder and more cunning and skilful in the business of smuggling. Dawood began to worship money and lust for more power. This turned him into a scheming, manipulative and self-centred don, unlike his predecessors.

Arguably, Dawood would be the only Indian don who took the mafia espionage to a totally different level. Long before phone tapping became a major weapon in the arsenal of the Bombay Police, Dawood exploited the medium to keep tabs on his friends and enemies. According to Dawood's cronies, the don had paid a substantial amount of money to a few technicians in the telephone exchange to pass on all recorded conversations on the telephone numbers he had wanted monitored. This gave him access to not only their hidden thoughts but also the advance intelligence to pre-empt events and act accordingly. Dawood thus managed to spy on his own men. The corporate czars and politicians of today actually picked this up much, much later.

Khalid and Dawood were quite close and it was their mutual ambition to make money and succeed that tied them together. However, Khalid and Dawood differed with each other on several issues. Khalid believed in old-school values and a code of honour, while for Dawood it was all about achieving what he had set out to achieve regardless of right or wrong. But the protégé was grateful to Khalid for the big break and the hand-holding. Both of them loved each other too much and, despite their differences, hung on together.

It was at this point that Khalid began partnering with Galadari, and Dawood aligned with the Pakistani syndicate. Soon the five-man army, which had already been truncated after the death of Sabir, was dissolved. Khalid and Dawood realized that they didn't want to become foes after such a strong friendship; they decided to amicably part ways. This farewell was so painful for Khalid that he decided to not only quit the syndicate but also the city. He relocated to Dubai and began working with the Galadari family, though he occasionally made trips to Bombay to keep in touch with his family.

Dawood, though he missed Khalid's pragmatic solutions, marched on to become the uncrowned king of the Bombay mafia. Now Dawood would never have to think twice or have to consult anyone about his decisions. He launched a new scheme of smuggling called 'partnership project'. This scheme allowed every investor to invest in any number of jackets in a particular speedboat; so people could invest in five to fifty jackets, depending on their financial capacity.

In Khalid's absence, Dawood embarked on a fresh chapter in gold smuggling. His idea was to cram the coffers full, at any cost. The plan was that if twenty people would get together to pool in their resources and order 200 jackets of gold biscuits, then all of them were expected to deposit the money with Dawood as he would be helming the operation coast to coast, right from Dubai and all the way to Bombay. There was a new excitement in the air, even small-time businessmen were hoping to join the big league and become smugglers. The jackets were loaded with gold biscuits in Dubai and the vessel was seemingly en route to Bombay.

Dawood told everyone that he would land the consignment in a week's time. However, after the said time passed, he called a meeting of all the investors. The situation seemed grim as Dawood dropped the bad news: '*Hamara maal* (Our goods) . . .' his voice trailed, '*Customs ne pakad liya* (Has been caught by customs),' he finished, his voice dropping in decibels.

A collective sigh of incredulity and denial rose in the room. Expressions like '*Nahin, bhai* (No, bhai)', '*Kya baat kar rahe ho* (What are you saying)?' and '*Ya mere Allah* (Oh Allah)!' filled the air. This was followed by agitated chatter and the whole room erupted like a flea market.

Dawood remained quiet for a while and then said, '*Bas karo, mera bhi nuqsan hua hai . . . Business mein nafa nuqsaan toh hota rehta hai . . . Aap sab ghar jaiyye* (Please stop, even I have been ruined . . . One experiences profits as well as losses in business . . . All of you please go home),' Dawood said in his attempts to placate them. No one was happy but they inferred that Dawood was apparently crushed with the loss and that it was better to leave him alone.

But no one knew the real story. Indian customs officials had received a tip-off about a small boat on its way to Bombay and seized it in Indian territorial waters. However, the boat had only twenty jackets, and neither had they been fully loaded, nor were all of them genuine gold. Some pockets also had counterfeit biscuits, thanks to the Pakistani syndicate's anticipation of the bust.

It was, in fact, an elaborate scam that Dawood along with the Pakistani cartel had pulled off with a devious subterfuge. Dawood had taken money from twenty investors, equivalent to 200 jackets, or 2000 kg of gold, which was an enormous amount of money. But if only a small amount of gold was confiscated and the news flashed everywhere, then all the investors could be conveniently told that their share was lost in the seizure. Dawood ended up having to share the spoils of only twenty jackets with the Pakistanis, which is barely 10 per cent of the entire turnover. The rest of the 90 per cent of the unaccounted cash came safely into his kitty, undivided and without any hassles.

Dawood swindled his investors a few more times using different mechanisms and a variety of ploys. Sometimes, instead of calling them all together, he would call them individually to inform them. After a few such instances, the investors got wiser and then stopped investing money with him altogether.

The Bombay cabal, which always hated Khalid's proximity to Dawood and felt jealous about his influence on the young gun, missed Khalid's presence, strangely. For the first time they realized that Khalid had made dealings transparent and scrupulous. They had never faced betrayal or deception with him.

Was this the reason that Dawood had wanted to split from Khalid? Did Dawood feel stymied with Khalid's decision-making and involvement in the business? Khalid was a hurdle for Dawood who desired total domination and unbridled access to money and control over people. Khalid would have played on Dawood's conscience and not have allowed these kinds of decoy dealings and looting of investors.

Khalid brought character to the mafia. His contention was that if smuggling is *tijarat* (business), then it should be conducted scrupulously and conscientiously. Not that Khalid did not get involved in violent skirmishes, but he ensured that he was never declared wanted by the law. He felt that he should never get in the way of the law in such a way that the cops come at him hammer and tongs. He didn't want to be a menace for the country.

Among the lessons Khalid imparted to Dawood that the latter never paid heed to was this: 'Despite all your failings and dalliances in crime, you can still remain a white-collar smuggler.'

It was adherence to this principle alone that kept Khalid safe and unharmed at the hands of the law. He kept making trips to Bombay, conducted business on a smaller scale and remained happy. There was never ever a lookout notice issued against him. However, Khalid, who normally had no regrets, nursed one major remorse all his life. He had lost his cool once and acted on an impulse. The incident had shaken him to the core.

In the meanwhile, the mafia got together in a huddle and began talking among themselves and decided to bring about a reconciliation between Khalid and Dawood. For them, the Khalid–Dawood combine was an expedient arrangement. But even before Dawood could react to such suggestions and overtures, things spiralled out of control for him. Dawood was declared wanted in too many cases and the cops were hot on his heels. He realized that he could not continue to live in Bombay and made a hasty escape from the city in 1986, minutes before the Bombay Police raided his Musafir Khana headquarters on Pakmodia Street in south Bombay.

Dawood relocated to Dubai for good, leaving no scope of a return. He recreated Bombay in Dubai, importing all his favourite people there, including film stars. The year 1993, however, changed his life. After the March 1993 serial blasts in Bombay, helmed by Tiger Memon, Dawood became a fugitive and had to soon leave Dubai and shift to Karachi. Once in Pakistan, the dynamics of his business plans and everything else underwent a sea change as he was no longer free in the real sense but watched always by the eagle eyes of the

Inter-Services Intelligence, better known as the ISI. For Dawood, the world had become a very small place, and he rued all his past mistakes as he pined for his motherland.

As they say, much of this was due to his own undoing.

But for Khalid, of course, the going was a little less rough.

25

Deception Point

Madhav Thakkar was totally confused, and desperate to save his own life. He had everything that a man could want to enjoy life comfortably. He had lots of money and nothing to fear from the underworld as he was well connected. Thakkar had an understanding with the underworld as well as with the police. Karim Lala and Dawood's former aide, Ejaz Pathan, were his close friends and, in fact, there were several Bombay Police officers in the top echelons who were on his speed dial. Thakkar had cultivated relationships with police officers in such a way that they responded to him promptly. This was quite a feat for any police informer.

Thakkar had nothing to worry about in his otherwise uneventful life until, one ordinary day, a few men barged into his office, sprayed bullets around indiscriminately, shattered each and every window and glass object in view, and then, just before decamping from the spot, lobbed two hand grenades into his office, which blew everything to smithereens. Thakkar was left frozen in horror for a long time after the attack.

The business district of Masjid Bunder in south Bombay, which is the hub of grain, spices and other grocery items and a wholesale market, was shaken by the attack. Such a ravaging assault was unprecedented in an otherwise chaotic but peaceful area of the city.

Thakkar was thanking his stars for surviving such a lethal attack completely unhurt, albeit by the skin of his teeth. When he saw the men whipping out their guns and opening fire at him, he dived and took cover behind a table, later rolling behind a steel almirah. This not only saved him from the volley of bullets but also the grenades. Incidentally, one of the grenades turned out to be a dud and did not explode. The other grenade that exploded did not injure him as it detonated at quite a distance.

Thakkar could not believe that he was completely unscathed in such a violent attack. He immediately began snooping around to find out who could have put out a contract on his life. He was utterly baffled when he found out that none of the dons wanted him dead, including Dawood, Chhota Rajan and even Arun Gawli. *Then who did this? And why?* Thakkar had no answers to any of these riddles.

Thakkar had been a police informer for years. This business of providing information to the police had given him plenty of clout. There are three kinds of snitches in the world. The first one provides information for money; this kind is considered unreliable. Then there is the reluctant informant, who is actually planted by the police or forced by them to share information. The informant has to provide tip-offs under duress and does it only for his own safety and the well-being of his family; this type of informer is not very useful but once in a while his information can help in gathering intelligence and getting vital leads in ongoing investigations. The last type of informer is the one who wants to take revenge on the enemy gang. This type of informer is the most reliable asset for the police. Ironically, Thakkar did not belong to any of the categories. The cops were, however, quite happy with him and he had them eating out of his hands.

Thakkar revelled in his connections and strutted around calling himself '*Madhav Bhai, mama ke mama*', which loosely means 'the uncle of the police'. (Policemen were pejoratively referred to as 'mamas' by everyone.) Madhav Bhai had no worries as his network was functioning smoothly. Thakkar kept obliging everyone and thought he was a big shot in the making.

However, sometimes, one small, unrelated incident can snowball into a major catastrophe and affect several lives. Thakkar could never have dreamt that his intervention in a business dispute would actually put him on the warpath against Khalid and sound the death knell for him.

An entrepreneur had procured an investment to the tune of half a million US dollars, which was the equivalent of more than 1 crore rupees, from a businessman named Kailash Agarwal. Agarwal had liked his business proposal and had raised the sum after mortgaging his house and car. Agarwal expected him to return the money with a handsome interest in a year's time, so he could repay his loan commitments. However, when the payment could not be made, Agarwal was pushed to the brink of bankruptcy and penury. The banks wanted to attach Agarwal's properties.

Agarwal began knocking on the doors of the police for help, but they refused to mediate saying that it was a civil dispute and that he should approach the courts for redressal and arbitration. Agarwal knew that the courts would be too busy and that by the time they finally got a chance to look into the matter, he would virtually be on the road with a begging bowl.

Suddenly, Agarwal was reminded of Khalid, who was obligated to him because Agarwal had once helped him financially; Khalid had then, in turn, promised to rescue him from a tight corner if he ever found himself in one. A despondent and desperate Agarwal reached out to Khalid. Khalid felt sorry for Agarwal's plight and decided to help him. He immediately dispatched his henchmen to the entrepreneur's house in Walkeshwar. But the man was not at home. Moreover, when he returned home he did not know why some ruffians had come looking for him. He called Thakkar, who immediately got in touch with the senior cops and got police protection for the businessman.

Here's the cruel twist that neither Thakkar nor his nemesis could have foreseen until it was too late. One of the goons who had gone to the entrepreneur's house was Shafi Toofani, who had been a dreaded mafia hitman working at the behest of Khalid. Toofani was also Khalid's ace lieutenant in Bombay.

When Toofani realized the speed with which the entrepreneur got police protection overnight, he understood that it was Thakkar's handiwork. Toofani was nursing an old grudge against Thakkar. He had heard that Thakkar was squealing on him and the police officers had now put him on the hit list for an encounter. Toofani hatched a clever plot to pre-empt the police action. The idea was so simple that it would not only save his life but would also eliminate Thakkar conveniently from the scheme of things.

Khalid was left stunned when he received a call from an irate Madhav Thakkar the next day. Thakkar showered a volley of abuses on Khalid and then openly challenged him to do whatever he could; the entrepreneur would not return the money. Thakkar's stinging, insolent attitude had Khalid riled up. He had never had so many expletives hurled at him.

Also, the temerity of Thakkar and his audacity to throw down the gauntlet at Khalid was astounding. Ganglords thrive on the business of fear. They always worry that their empire will collapse if people stop fearing them.

Khalid wanted to make an example of Thakkar. He instructed his men to leave the entrepreneur and prioritize killing Thakkar instead; he told them the lesson imparted should be so loud and shrill that even his deaf detractors should be able to hear it. The diktat was clear: kill Thakkar and crush him. It was with this decree that the men used machine guns and grenades in the attack.

Thakkar was running helter-skelter and desperately trying to figure out who could be so furious with him. Who would use a bomb to kill a man after such a burst of bullets, Thakkar often wondered. He also knew that the underworld shooters normally fired at point-blank range and often took headshots, which invariably proved fatal. Thakkar stopped going to office and confined himself to his house in the north-eastern suburb of Ghatkopar East. He hired over forty bodyguards and surrounded himself with enough security at all times. He stopped stepping out of the house except for extremely important errands like visiting a doctor.

A panic-stricken Thakkar also began to travel with a helmet on at all times, including in his bullet-proof car. This made him the subject of ridicule in his business and social circles. But Thakkar had survived a brutal attack and he alone knew the ferocity unleashed on him by the assailants. In the meanwhile, Khalid was furious that Thakkar had escaped the attack. This time, Khalid instructed ten men to follow Thakkar and pump bullets into him until he stopped breathing.

Thakkar had not yet recovered from his earlier nightmare, but the incessant mocking from the people around forced him to drop the helmet. One day, in June 1992, at 9.20 p.m., when Thakkar left his house and was passing by Mulund East, his car was intercepted by two handcarts. One man struck the car windscreen with a crowbar, while the other broke a window and indiscriminately fired at Thakkar. The gunmen kept shooting at his body until the last iota of life was drained out of him. The police extracted nineteen bullets from his body. The brutality of the killing sent shockwaves through the city and in police circles.

Khalid was satisfied with his sharpshooters' execution. But he did not gloat over the killing and instead experienced a strange nagging feeling, one he had never felt earlier. Khalid began to wonder why he wasn't getting that feeling of satisfaction on punishing an intransigent man. There was no history of animosity between the two of them. Why would Thakkar, without provocation, behave in such a haughty and disdainful manner? Khalid spent days digging for answers; he subsequently gave up and occupied himself in other engagements. However, one day, the answer himself walked into Khalid's life when he received a call from Madhav Thakkar.

Khalid felt the earth move beneath his feet. Madhav Thakkar was dead. His army of shooters had killed Thakkar. His body had been identified by the police and reported extensively by the newspapers. Thakkar could not possibly be alive, let alone make a phone call to Khalid. Even stranger, Thakkar seemed to be bawling over the phone and begging for his forgiveness. The non-stop crying was making it difficult to decipher what Thakkar was trying to plead for, until it suddenly started making sense to Khalid.

'I am not Madhav Thakkar but Talha Ansari; I masqueraded as Thakkar on the phone and challenged and abused you. Please forgive me,' said the caller, full of guilt.

Khalid began to turn blue with rage, when Talha's parents came on the line and began imploring him to spare the life of their young son. Khalid then controlled his anger and started asking questions. Why did he behave in this irresponsible manner? Why play a prank that put someone's life on the line?

Talha told Khalid that it was Shafi Toofani who had forced him to call Khalid and impersonate Thakkar. Talha had not known about the consequences of the call. Toofani had assured Talha that they were only playing some mischief on Khalid. Talha did not know about Thakkar and had never anticipated the repercussions. Khalid replaced the phone in the cradle and let out a thundering shriek. He was more contrite about killing a man than being furious about being deceived by his own top shooter, and such a manipulative betrayal at that.

Toofani knew that Khalid did not forgive anyone who used abusive language towards him. Also, if someone dared Khalid to a task, then Khalid would never allow the man to get away after cocking a snook at him. For him, the only convenient and inexpensive way of getting rid of his bête noire Thakkar was to unleash Khalid's wrath on him.

Toofani threatened Talha at gunpoint in his parents' presence into calling up Khalid and pretending to be Thakkar. For Talha, it was a matter of making one phone call and saving the life of his parents and himself. But when he read about Thakkar's violent end, they all got scared for their lives. They shivered at the thought of Khalid ever realizing that he had been fooled by a hoodwinker. After spending days in fear of retribution, they decided that it was better to confess to Khalid than allowing for the possibility of forcing him to hunt them down after he realized the truth.

Khalid wanted to punish Toofani as well, but he had gone underground since the killing. Toofani had miscalculated the whole game plan. He thought that Thakkar's killing would get him off the radar of the cops. But he did not account for the fact that the Bombay Police would only intensify their pursuit. And if earlier he would have been thrown in jail after being charged under a stringent act, Thakkar's killing would only multiply his problems manifold.

Even as Khalid was looking for Toofani, the Bombay Police got to him and killed him in an encounter.

Thakkar's killing had singed Khalid so badly that he spent months in remorse. Khalid also vowed to never order anyone's killing again and bid adieu to all involvement in mafia activities. Until 1992, Khalid used to make incognito trips to Bombay, but after the Thakkar–Toofani debacle, Khalid retreated into his shell and sought to be a recluse, though he remained in touch with his relatives.

Khalid was in hibernation for over twenty-five years until I decided to establish contact with him and convinced him to answer my questions.

26

The End of the Line

23 April 2018

Park Regis Kris Kin Hotel, Dubai-Karamah

Khalid walks into the lobby and warmly shakes hands with Rayyan and me. Until now, we have been invariably summoned to a venue of his choice, always escorted by some beefy, dour-looking men. Today, Khalid insisted on meeting us at the place where I was staying in Dubai. Initially, I tried to dissuade him, but after initial resistance, I agreed. Khalid reached on time, around 3 p.m., and to my surprise he had no acolytes with him.

Khalid took a seat in the coffee shop and we immediately got down to discuss my last few remaining queries with him as I had to leave for the airport to board a 5.40 p.m. Emirates flight to Mumbai. From my earlier experience of dealing with dangerous men, I had always noticed that they decided to meet me a couple of hours before my departure from the city and then delayed me in such a manner that I missed my flight.

However, we resolved to be brief and wrap up the conversation quickly.

The conversation started on an unsettling note. Khalid abruptly began the story of his man Prakash in Bandra in Mumbai.

'Prakash was my landing agent in Bombay and I used to trust him immensely. But once, when I sent gold in a launch, he played dirty with me. He safely packed the gold biscuits in a bag, tied them in a fishing net and concealed it below the boat, so that it could not be detected by the customs sleuths. His people on the coast were able to see that the vessel had reached the landing spots empty.

'Prakash then told me that customs has seized the gold. I was disheartened but then I found out through my own intelligence machinery that Prakash was deceiving me to usurp all the gold biscuits on the boat. I could not forgive this treachery of a man I trusted so much.

'I issued instructions to my hit squad in Bombay to take him out in a manner that it became a lesson for others.

'*Gaddari ki saza maut hai* (Death is the punishment for betrayal),' said Khalid, concluding the story.

This emphatic punchline was delivered with such intensity and purpose that not only a battle-scarred pen-pusher like me but even a young man like Rayyan could interpret it to convey a subtle threat to us. However, both of us pretended to remain calm and unfazed.

Khalid was trying to debate that I should desist from the mention of his unsuccessful foray into Bollywood. However, he agreed when I explained to him the rationale behind the narrative.

He claimed that there was no Red Corner Notice against him and that he had given up smuggling in 1992. He also explained that he had never been involved in any anti-national activities. But Khalid was wary of returning to Mumbai as he did not want to become a trophy for some trigger-happy cop.

I asked him whether he had ever diversified into drug trafficking after quitting smuggling. Khalid vehemently denied having to do anything with the drugs business.

Rayyan showed him a news report about Khalid Ghaswalla's arrest at the Dubai International Airport last year. 'I think it must be somebody else. Howsoever rich or influential you are in Dubai, you cannot do business with drugs and remain safe from the law. Look at what happened to Vicky Goswami despite his legitimate front as a hotelier. The moment the authorities found out about his involvement in drugs, he was busted and thrown behind bars.' Goswami was the owner of the Empire group of hotels, dotting several cities on the globe. He subsequently married Bollywood starlet Mamta Kulkarni. The Thane police recently registered cases against both of them.

If Khalid was not into smuggling, drugs or any illegal activities now, then what were his current businesses? Or was this just a smokescreen? Khalid explained that until last year he was dabbling in the hotel business and had stakes in Hotel George in partnership with the late Abdul Wahab's son Ilyaas. But when he realized that it was not as lucrative an enterprise as he thought it would be, he moved on to other businesses.

Khalid said he is now associated with the ambitious 40-billion-dollar construction project called the City of Arabia. The project is the brainchild of Wahab's enterprising sons Ilyaas and Mustafa Galadari. 'We are still close and have family-like bonds with each other,' Khalid said.

What about Khalid's own family then? He is reluctant to talk about them. 'My sons are well-educated men settled in

European capitals and have got nothing to do with my past,' Khalid avers mysteriously.

What about his relationship with Dawood? 'Oh, he is still dear to me, like my own brother. We both share a special bond and he has profound respect for me. I was invited for his daughter's wedding in Pakistan but I could not make it. We do keep in touch occasionally for old times' sake,' he said.

Khalid claimed that his last meeting with Dawood was in 1990 and that they have not met since then, though they have spoken over the phone a couple of times.

The conversation had become longer than I expected and Rayyan got anxious that I would get late for my flight. He indicated that I should wind up and leave. There were still so many questions and so many intricate puzzles that needed to be answered. But I did not want to miss my flight.

I asked my final question, before getting up to leave.

'Don't you feel like returning to India? Don't you yearn to see Mumbai, the city of your dreams and aspirations, and breathe the air of Harda and Bhopal, the towns that gave you your identity?'

The question really made him emotional and nostalgic, and I could see tears welling up in his eyes. There was a slight constriction in his throat as he tried to gather his thoughts and speak.

'Of course, I want to return to India. Who doesn't want to spend his life in his homeland? My ancestors might have come from Batkhela, but for me India is my country. I will come when I feel the time is conducive and I will not be ill-treated by the authorities,' Khalid said, struggling to articulate his feelings.

I thought we were done. Both Rayyan and I rose. But Khalid was not.

'I really want to return to the country before I die. This is one unfulfilled desire of mine. I hope I can make it,' he added.

We shook hands warmly.

I hastily bid him goodbye and felt my heart racing. Right now my motherland beckoned, and here I was, still in this lobby, seeing crucial moments slipping away.

Rayyan showed amazing agility, took my bags and jumped behind the wheel of his Prado. As he sped on the clean, well-navigated roads of Dubai, I felt like I was being driven by Jason Statham in *The Transporter*.

Alhamdulillah!

This time I did not miss my flight after meeting a dangerous man, though I was the last one to board the aircraft.

List of Sources

Chapter 1: The Pathan Threat

The primary source of information was personal interviews conducted with Khalid Pehelwan in his Dubai office. However, the information was substantiated with other interviews that I had conducted during the course of my earlier books like *Dongri to Dubai*.

Chapter 2: Reel vs Real

Kamal Chadha is a known history-sheeter and an accused in various cases. A variety of cases has been registered against him at the Directorate of Revenue Intelligence (DRI) and the special cell of Delhi police. One such dossier was read out to me by an officer in the Delhi Police, and I had taken notes from the same.

Chadha has also been a subject of consistent reportage in news reports, which I referred to while writing this chapter. Two such reports are mentioned here:

Sachin Parashar, 'Dawood aide gives Delhi cops a slip', *Times of India*, 1 May 2005, https://bit.ly/2N0nIKs, accessed 20 July 2018.

Sachin Parashar, 'Dawood's friend in Delhi probed for match-fixing', *Times of India*, 9 February 2007, https://bit.ly/2tjAaMk, accessed 20 July 2018.

The portions about Sanjay Gupta seeking help from Chadha have come directly from him during his interview. This also includes Gupta's conversation with Chhota Shakeel en route to Shirdi. The conversation is reproduced verbatim in my book *Dongri to Dubai: Six Decades of the Mumbai Mafia* (New Delhi: Lotus Collection, 2012).

Chapter 3: The Fall of Sabir

This entire chapter is sourced from Khalid Pehelwan's interview, wherein he added details to the story. The incident was earlier described in *Dongri to Dubai*.

Chapter 4: The First Lead

The main source for the chapter is Mr Sikandar Shah, Khalid Khan's ace lieutenant in Mumbai. However, Sikandar's criminal activities, in complicity with Karim Lala, had been registered at the Nagpada police station by then police inspector Shamsher Khan Pathan in 1984.

The infamous incident of the arrest of Judge J.W. Singh under the Maharashtra Control of Organised Crime Act (MCOCA) was widely reported. The killing of advocate Liyaqat Ali Shaikh by Chhota Shakeel and the underworld–legal nexus was featured in newspapers and magazines:

Sheela Raval, 'Revelation of nexus between judge and underworld don shakes legal circles', *India Today*, 20 September 1999, https://bit.ly/2N0fq5p, accessed 2 May 2018.

Chapter 5: The Dubai Rendezvous

This chapter is a result of my personal interaction with Khalid and the way I was taken to meet him. At the time I was accompanied by Rayyan Rizvi, my nephew and young friend, who transcribed the entire interview for me.

Chapter 6: The Legend of Pathans

Haroon Rashid, *History of the Pathans* (Islamabad: Haroon Rashid, 2002).

Chapter 7: The Challenger

The wrestling-match incident is described at length by both Khalid and Sikandar. Parts of it were substantiated by a few retired cops and former members of the mafia.

Chapter 8: The Protégé

Retired assistant commissioner of police Burhan Malgi was a family friend of Head Constable Ibrahim Kaskar. Since he was Kaskar's senior, he was sympathetic to his problems and tried to help him. Malgi was also a well-informed source about the Bombay underworld. Most of the information about the family and Dawood's earlier struggles comes from him.

S. Hussain Zaidi, *Dongri to Dubai: Six Decades of the Mumbai Mafia* (New Delhi: Lotus Collection, 2012).

Chapter 9: Khalid: Bashu's Acolyte

This piece of information was narrated to me by two journalists of Urdu newspapers, on the condition of anonymity. Subsequently, when I double-checked with Khalid Pehelwan, he verified parts of the said information. I have also referred to the book by Sharafat Khan:

Sharafat Khan, *Underworld King Dawood Ibrahim and Gang War* (Mumbai: Sharafat Khan, N.D.).

Chapters 10–14

The entire source for the chapters is interview-based, and I have conducted several sessions of interviews with ACP Malgi, Dawood's aides in Mumbai and crime branch officers who did not wish to be quoted. This material was then cross-checked with Khalid when I met him.

Prabhu Chawla, 'Law Enforcement Agencies Make Record Seizures of Gold', *India Today*, 31 Oct 1988, https://bit.ly/2ByJroC, accessed 20 July 2018.

Chapter 15: The Bashu–Khalid Split

The information and description for this chapter have come from senior officers of the DRI.

Chapter 16: The Art of Smuggling

The background information on Antulay's politics and social interactions has been sourced from several Urdu and Marathi newspapers.

Several anecdotes were shared with me by former journalist turned Shiv Sena leader Pramod Navalkar. Navalkar also told me about Antulay's reformation in the community and crackdown on liquor dens.

'Former Maharashtra CM AR Antulay passes away', *Times of India*, 2 December 2014, https://bit.ly/2TJHhJJ.

Deepak Lokhande, 'The rise and fall of former Maharashtra Chief Minister AR Antulay', *DNA*, 2 December 2014, https://bit.ly/2Buw6gR, accessed 27 June 2018.

Chapter 17: Dawood's Overtures

The information was given to me by Dawood's brother Sabir Kaskar before he was arrested under the MCOCA.

Chapter 18: The Five-Man Army

This is an interview-based chapter on my meeting with Khalid. However, the Galadari-related information has come from Middle Eastern and Indian magazines. I have relied heavily on *India Today*'s detailed feature on him:

Sumit Mitra, 'Abdul Latif Galadari Surfaces in India as Govt Withdraws Smuggling Cases against the Brothers', *India Today*, 29 October 2013, https://bit.ly/2RTySBA, accessed 20 January 2018.

Chapter 19: An Undercover Wedding

The information in this book has been sourced from different published materials including the compilation titled 'Growth of Gangsterism in the City' by former Mumbai police commissioner Mahesh Narain Singh and several other dossiers. Several pieces were put together to build the chapter. I have sourced the rest from *Dongri to Dubai* and Khalid's interview.

Chapter 20: The D-Gang

The incident was sourced from a police dossier of the Mumbai crime branch, while background on Antulay was gathered from a *Times of India* article:

'Former Maharashtra CM AR Antulay passes away', *Times of India*, 2 December 2014, https://bit.ly/2TJHhJJ.

Most of the information about the Gujarat incident with Dawood and related episodes was gleaned from the following book by former Delhi police commissioner Neeraj Kumar:

Neeraj Kumar, *Dial D for Don: Inside Stories of CBI Missions* (Gurgaon: Penguin Random House, 2015).

R.S. Nayak vs A.R. Antulay, 16 February 1984
1984 AIR 684, 1984 SCR (2) 495

Chapter 21: Musa Ka Ghoosa

The incident had many narrators, including ACP Malgi, veterans of the crime branch, the people present at Tardeo market and a relative of Mehmood Kalia. These accounts were then subsequently confirmed by Khalid Pehelwan.

Chapter 22: The Gold 'Wave'

The main sources for the chapter include an officer of the DRI, former crime branch officers and Sikandar Shah, who used to be an aide of Khalid Pehelwan.

Chapter 23: An Amicable Parting

Shiv Sena's issue of Sons of the Soil is their main political plank.

'For Sena, it's "son-of-soil" agenda over Hindutva', *Times of India*, 26 June 2007, https://bit.ly/2DwGhSb, accessed 5 May 2018.

'Dubai tycoon Abdul Wahab Galadari loses global business empire', *India Today*, 15 January 1984, https://bit.ly/2TOp4eh, accessed 20 May 2018.

Chapter 24: 'Never Get Caught'

The information for this chapter was gleaned through interviews conducted with several members of the Dawood gang who had witnessed this incident with their own eyes.

Chapter 25: Deception Point

The information for this chapter was gleaned through the interview conducted with Khalid Pehelwan wherein he described the whole incident.

Chapter 26: The End of the Line

The information for this chapter was gleaned from my personal interactions in the Dubai hotel.

About the Author

S. Hussain Zaidi is India's number-one crime writer. He is a veteran of investigative, crime and terror reporting. He is the author of several bestselling books, including *Dangerous Minds, Dongri to Dubai: Six Decades of the Mumbai Mafia, My Name Is Abu Salem* and *Black Friday*. He has worked for the *Asian Age, Mumbai Mirror, Mid-Day* and the *Indian Express*. He is also the associate producer for the HBO movie *Terror in Mumbai,* based on the 26/11 terror strikes. He lives with his family in Mumbai.